BUILDING COMMUNITY
in Youth Groups

BY DENNY RYDBERG
with Robin Dursch and Ken Beebe

Group
Books
Loveland, Colorado

120267

DEDICATION

To every youth worker who is dedicated to helping
his or her collection of individuals
become a committed community.

Building Community in Youth Groups

Credits

Edited by Cindy S. Hansen
Designed by Jean Bruns
Illustrations by Ric Soulen
Cover photo by Ron Meyer

Library of Congress Cataloging-in-Publication Data

Rydberg, Denny.
    Building community in youth groups.

    1. Church group work with youth. I. Dursch, Robin, 1956-   . II. Beebe,
Ken, 1960-   . III. Title. BV4447.R93 1985   259′.2   85-17645
ISBN 0-931-529-06-9

Printed in the United States of America

FOREWORD

It is exciting to see how "group building" has become an accepted strategy in religious education. I can remember the day when it was only an "itch" in the minds of a few of us—struggling to find a way to make the church more loving.

With this book, the "group building" model has taken another step toward maturity—combining good learning theory with practical learning exercises. Denny Rydberg and his friends, Ken Beebe and Robin Dursch, have done a great job of taking from the past and adding their own contemporary focus and personality.

This book offers a five-step plan for effective community building in youth groups: bond building, opening up, affirming, stretching, and deeper sharing and goal setting. This plan uses over 100 easy-to-follow exercises with discussion questions. This book has a great deal of material to help youth workers crack the barriers between young people and then develop relationships of trust and caring.

Denny describes a vision for his own youth group: "I'd like to see the body of Christ, the 'forever family of God,' become a reality in my group. I'd like a 'family feel' to characterize my group. I want *everyone* to feel cared for and loved. I want the participants to feel that the youth group is a place (maybe even *the* place) where they can share their deepest joys and sorrows. I'd like to see them maturing in their relationship to Christ, to each other and to the world. I'd like the students to understand and experience joy and fun. I want them to be able to honestly say: 'I'm glad I'm part of this group. It means so much to me.' "

All youth workers have a similar dream for their youth group. Used correctly, I see this book offering youth leaders an excellent tool to use to reach their dream of a Christlike, caring group.

Here's to the dream!
Here's to the future church!
Here's to a great book!

Lyman Coleman
Serendipity House

ACKNOWLEDGMENTS

Denny wants to thank his wife, Marilyn, his old sidekick Lyman Coleman, and the rest of the National Youth Ministry Team who several years ago inspired this book: Gary Downing, Paul Evans, Jane Holslag and Tim Hansel.

Ken wants to acknowledge one of his former professors Mike Allen and a good friend Jim LeShana.

Robin is grateful to the Christian education department of Biola, to the staff of Sea and Summit and to the staff of Wilderness Trails.

Both Ken and Robin also want to thank their boss, Paul Evans.

All of us would like to thank the Reachout staff: Mark Eaton, Bill Schaarschmidt, Bob Bavis and the numerous summer staff.

And finally, we would like to thank our competent project editor, Cindy Hansen, and the editor of Group Books, Lee Sparks.

"Fantasy Island" and "Magic Pawnshop" were adapted from: Sue Forbess-Greene, L.M.S.W., **The Encyclopedia of Icebreakers**, San Diego, CA: University Associates, Inc., 1983. Used by permission.

"Character Strength Tree" was adapted from material in **Teaching People to Love Themselves**, by Dov Peretz Elkins (Rochester, NY: Growth Associates).

"Faces of Me" poem by Verne Becker. Copyright © 1983 CAMPUS LIFE Magazine, Christianity Today, Inc. Used by permission.

Many thanks to Reachout Expeditions, P.O. Box 464, Anacortes, WA 98221.

CONTENTS

INTRODUCTION

So you have a youth group.

So do I.

And although you and I don't work together, we both have visions and dreams for what we would like to see happen with our youth group members.

What do you want to see happen with your group? What vision for the present and the future pushes you onward? What do you want to see the group become?

In the past, I never considered myself much of a visionary and dreamer. But as I grow older, I know that I'm becoming more of a dreamer. Various dreams, visions and pictures come to my mind as I think about "my group."

I'd like to see the body of Christ, the "forever family of God," become a reality in my group. I'd like a "family feel" to characterize my group. I want *everyone* to feel cared for and loved. I want the participants to feel that the youth group is a place (maybe even *the* place) where they can share their deepest joys and sorrows. I want the students to develop at least two or three intimate, caring friendships. These friends would be the kind who get out of bed at 1 a.m. if necessary to help in a crisis. I want a newcomer to feel at home, where no one can distinguish the "in" group from the "out" group.

I'd also like to see the group members excited about their relationship with Jesus Christ, open with their questions, enthusiastic about their faith, feeling comfortable in the group so that they can share their excitement at one meeting or be as subdued as they want at another meeting without feeling like a second-class Christian. I'd like the students to know more about the person of Jesus Christ. And I'd like their Christian faith not to be a *religion*, but a lifelong, dynamic, growing, maturing *relationship* with the Lord of their lives.

I'd like to see the youth group members excited about making a difference in the world. I want them to discover their unique gifts and abilities, and desire to use them to advance the kingdom. I envision young people having compassion for the hurting and dispossessed and using their creativity and commitment to make a difference in the world. I'd like to see them increasing in wisdom, stature, and favor with God and others. I'd like to see them maturing in their relationship to Christ, to each other and to the world.

I'd like the students to understand and experience joy and fun. I want them to be able to honestly say: "I'm glad I'm part of this group. It means so much to me."

That's the ideal. The vision. The aim. Some of your dreams may be similar to mine, but the reality of the situation is that most groups aren't like our dreams. In fact, for many churches, the word "group" should not be used. Perhaps some of the following names would be more appropriate: youth mob, youth crowd, youth assembly, youth individuals, youth division, youth collection. But not "youth group." Not yet.

Why do youth groups vary so wildly? Why is one group loving and kind while another group down the street is a put-down festival? The reason is that our youth groups are inherently complex. Dynamics exist that make it easier for students to be a collection of self-conscious individuals rather than a committed group. Whether the group consists of five people, 15, 50 or 500, the same potentially divisive-creating dynamics exist.

For instance, there's the dynamic of **leadership**. All groups have one to three people who surface as leaders. Regardless if they were elected to a youth group office, they lead by influence. Some of these leaders are mature and they help the collection become a group. Others are not. They "help" whatever semblance of a group you have become more of a collection of individuals. You also have some followers. They are ready to follow the leadership almost anywhere, any time. And then, you probably have a few rebels. They're not willing to follow anyone anywhere. To involve the rebels as a part of a group requires a special strategy (the five-step process of building community which we will describe in this book).

Then there's the dynamic of **motivation**. Some individuals attend the group because they have been forced to by well-meaning parents. Some are there because of romance. They're interested in a member of the opposite sex and the youth group meeting provides one more chance to develop that relationship. Some are there because they're bored and would do anything to get out of the house. Some are there because they've been brought by a friend but they have little knowledge of what the church, youth group, or Christian faith is all about. Some young people really want to be at youth group. They are intrinsically motivated. The hours spent with the group members are important times (maybe the most important times) in the week for them. Their friends are there; their identity is tied to the group; they belong; it's a second home that may be for them better than their first; they are part of the "in" group. But this in itself has some dangers. The others who are not part of the "in" group know it;

and they feel bad. These outsiders are torn between wanting to become part of the insiders and wanting to leave the group altogether.

Other dynamics are **desire** and **ability**. Some people want to learn about God and their relationship with him. Some don't. And for some, it doesn't matter. Some are willing to share what's on their minds and are sufficiently articulate to do so. They're not intimidated by speaking in front of the group. Some even enjoy it. And some monopolize any discussion time. But even these verbal youth often choke up when it comes to sharing deep feelings and inner thoughts. Others feel overwhelmed and can't share concepts or feelings aloud. They want to be accepted. They're desperately afraid of looking like a fool. So they almost always remain silent.

There's also the diverse **emotional** and **spiritual condition** of the individuals with whom you minister. Some have deep hurts and intense scars. They'd like some help but they are afraid to open up and so they cover the hurts and scars with activity. The youth group becomes a Band-Aid instead of a cure for them. Some are feeling pretty good. Life has gone well for them this week. But down inside, they have a few gnawing insecurities about themselves, their ability to relate with others, their identity, their future. But their feelings are not overwhelming and, although they could be helped in these areas, they don't desperately need immediate help.

Another dynamic is **energy**. Some students are almost clinically hyperactive; they can't sit still. Lectures are out with these people; their attention span is too low. Others are mature and they can listen and respond. However, these mature youth cannot listen and respond very well when the active students are causing disruptions.

That, friends, is diversity: dynamics with divisive potential.

But in each youth group, there are common elements that can be used to draw people together. The individuals are all working through adolescence. They are concerned with their bodies. Their minds are maturing and expanding. They look forward to adventure. They want (and need) independence from parents and other adults, but they need the guidance of those older than themselves. They feel that few people understand them and they want to be understood. They are searching for a personal identity and want "a place to stand." They want a practical religion that works. They all are gifted. They all are loved in God's sight. They all have great potential. They all experience tremendous peer pressure and a need to be part of something. In conscious and subconscious ways, they all battle with loneliness and restlessness and seek to overcome these feelings.

The key for a youth group leader is to build community: Use the common elements of the group members to overcome the diverse elements. Create a community from a collection of individuals. That's not easy.

Youth ministry is complicated, but not overwhelming. Despite the diversity of dissimilarly motivated individuals at different stages in their life, a common ground exists for the collection of individuals to become a healthy group. The "right stuff" is there for the group to become all we as youth leaders want it to become and more! It *is* possible to be a healthy family where hurts and joys are shared, where everyone feels welcome and known, and where discussion and learning take place.

However, the collection won't become a community automatically, naturally or unconsciously. A collection of individuals becomes a group as the Holy Spirit meets the individuals and makes them into a family. But there are conditions that we can create where this "building community" can take place.

God has partially entrusted us to help this diverse band of individuals become all that he wants them to be. In the process of building community, we can create an environment where all students can feel a part of a family, grow in their faith, discover their gifts, and help change the world. That's what this book is all about.

The idea for this book was conceived several years ago. Five of us who had been working with students for almost 20 years each (I can't believe I'm that old!) were meeting in a conference room at the Seattle-Tacoma International Airport. Gary Downing, a pastor from Minneapolis; Paul Evans, director of Youth Dynamics in Anacortes, Washington; Tim Hansel, president of Summit Expedition in San Dimas, California; my wife, Marilyn, and I were planning a series of 48 seminars across the United States on the subject of youth ministry. As we planned, we talked about the needs of youth workers and youth groups (some of which I've already described in this chapter) and brainstormed ways we could address those needs.

We began to discuss a term Tim Hansel had coined, "non-neutral learning." Our definition of non-neutral learning was: an active learning environment where everyone is forced to participate and thereby forced to learn.

An active learning environment isn't a "militarily" forced environment filled with rewards and punishments to instill learning. It is, however, an environment that is filled with so much fun or so many challenges that each student can't help but become a participant, a part of the group and a learner.

The more the five of us talked, the more we discovered how

similar our youth ministry approaches were and how much all of us were working at creating active learning environments in each of our geographically widespread ministries. We decided we would do more research, develop an approach, and compile effective strategies for creating this active learning environment for other youth workers to utilize in their ministries.

I assigned a great deal of the research to Robin Dursch and Ken Beebe, two of Paul Evans' staff workers who are active learning strategists and who are specializing in a part of Youth Dynamics—Reachout Expeditions. Reachout Expeditions uses wilderness camping to provide personal growth through group building. The exercises in this book have been adapted from the five-level philosophy of building community which Reachout uses in its year-round adventure programs.

Robin and Ken also work with kids in a more traditional setting and had brought the "wilderness" to the youth group meeting room. Robin and Ken were the catalysts in honing the five-step strategy you will find in **Building Community in Youth Groups**. These steps build on each other and eventually lead to action and changed lives: bond building, opening up, affirming, stretching, and deeper sharing and goal setting. The diagram on the following page illustrates these five steps.

As you read this book, you'll understand what these steps involve and how they work together. Plus, you'll incorporate into your ministry a catalog of more than 100 exercises that you can use to build your group.

Specific instructions are given at the beginning of each chapter that are essential to the success of these activities. Please read the instructions before you proceed. In addition, the last few chapters are designed to help you organize the strategies into events such as youth group meetings and retreats.

Although some of the activities in this book could be called "games," we prefer to call them "strategies" or "exercises" because of the connotation of the word "game." For example, "Games are just for fun," "Games are what you use at the start of the meeting as a crowdbreaker," etc.

We prefer to call the activities "exercises" or "strategies" because they help create an environment where people learn and where group building occurs. The strategies should not be confined to the beginning of a meeting as a "crowdbreaker." The strategies can be used depending on what you want them to accomplish: at the beginning of a meeting, in the middle, at the end, as the whole meeting, as part of the meeting, as part of a retreat, as the whole retreat, etc.

When you lead these exercises, you may feel anxious about

moving from the lecture method to a more experiential, active method. With the lecture method you know what you're going to say. With an active method you have less control over the outcome—what will be said and what people will learn. But that's part of the fun of trusting the Holy Spirit.

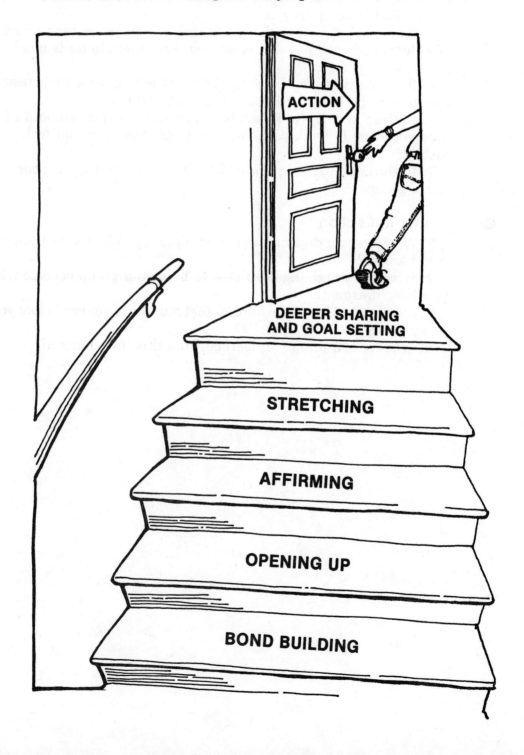

Some of you, as well as your students, may have an aversion to what you refer to as "game playing." If that's the case, I suggest that when you begin to use these exercises, you do the following:

1. *Begin with a non-threatening strategy.* Look at the bond building exercises in Chapter 2 and select the most non-threatening strategy *to you.*

2. *Be honest.* Admit to the youth that you've never been much of a "game player" but that what you want them to do is much more than a game.

3. *Be enthusiastic and involved.* Others who have similar reservations will be helped by observing your enthusiasm.

4. *Proceed slowly.* God has given you just the right amount of time you need to work with your students. You need not feel rushed.

With those thoughts in mind, let's build community in your youth group.

Questions for Reflection

1. What are your dreams for your youth group? What would you like it to become?

2. What are you doing right now to help your group become what you have dreamed?

3. What do you see as the hurdles that must be overcome before your group really becomes a family?

4. What is one thing you learned from this introduction?

CHAPTER 1:
BUILDING COMMUNITY

Scene One

The youth leader sighs. Her small group of six ninth grade girls are at each other's throats again. She has been meeting with them every Thursday afternoon at 3:30 for the past three months for the purpose of Bible study, prayer and sharing. But instead of a facilitator, she feels like a referee. The girls harp on each other's flaws yet know 1 Corinthians 13 by heart. "Where is the close, unified group I imagined myself leading?" the leader thinks. "Why don't the girls care about one another?"

Scene Two

The leader stands in front of the 20 youth group members and pours out his heart and thoughts about the desperate need for serving others. For 20 minutes he shares the message that took him three hours to prepare. But the students seem oblivious to his efforts. One student glances at her watch; another whispers to a friend; another points to a guy beginning to doze off; two giggle. The leader sighs as he completes his message and some of his zest of youth ministry dies.

Scene Three

Pete, a sophomore, has recently recovered from a bout with cancer. In front of his peers, he begins for the first time to share the physical and emotional strain of his struggle. For an hour, the youth group laughs and cries with Pete as he tells of his radiation treatments, the loss of his hair and how he felt about almost dying. As the meeting concludes and the students head home, both Pete and the group feel good; they've grown and become closer because he's been vulnerable and open with them. But Pete wonders and wishes he could have shared earlier *when* he was going through the battle instead of *after* he has survived.

Scene Four

Shari, a junior, wants to share Christ with her non-Christian friend Debbie who sits behind her in English class. More than once Shari has approached Debbie but has always backed away from talking about God because of a strong fear of rejection. Finally, Shari tells the youth group about her struggle. Group members reassure her by sharing their own similar frustrations. The group members pray that Shari will have the boldness to share the next time an opportunity arises. They help her come up with ideas on how best to communicate Christ to Debbie. With this added support and encouragement from her peers, Shari shares with Debbie three days later what Jesus means to her.

All these scenes are true. Names have been changed to protect the innocent and the guilty. For most of us, the first and second scenes are all too familiar. Some of us may have experienced the third scene. We all long for more experiences similar to the fourth scene. Like us, many youth leaders are forced to wonder why students don't experience true fellowship. Why do youth spend time together on Sunday but ignore each other at school on Monday? Why do they sing songs about the "family of God" yet hunger for the care and attention they are not experiencing in the group? Why do prayer requests, when finally given, focus only on ill relatives rather than on personal trials and victories?

We know that the Bible talks about burden bearing. Paul delivers a command from God, "Bear one another's burdens, and so fulfill the law of Christ" (Galatians 6:2). The Bible clearly mandates that Christians are to develop intimate friendships with one another, "Rejoice with those who rejoice, weep with those who weep" (Romans 12:15). But fellowship and community are more than potlucks and volleyball. Community is the weaving of lives into the body of Christ—building each other up, sharing joys and sorrows, caring about each other's needs and holding one another accountable. We know that. But how can we help individuals become a community where vulnerable group members feel free to share and bear one another's burdens?

Chuck Miller, a veteran youth worker, defines vulnerability as "choosing to share something about yourself that cannot be readily seen such as hopes, dreams, fears, embarrassments, joys and sorrows." This level of sharing is crucial to building community; however, vulnerability is not the end product. Vulnerability just for the sake of being vulnerable is not profitable. Sharing deeply is only beneficial when it is used as a means to bring about personal and spiritual growth.

Alcoholics Anonymous has made honesty and vulnerability indispensable in its work. AA members contend that the first step toward healing comes when a person publicly admits he or she has a problem. This happens in a youth group, too. When a student "talks out" a problem, healing begins. Potential solutions sometimes begin to surface; hope is renewed; support is expressed; and the input received through disclosure causes growth.

Once a student shares a concern, however, the youth group members must rally around him or her and show they care—despite the failures and imperfections that have been disclosed. If students don't feel free to fail, pharisaical facades begin to crop up in the group as members mask their true identities while inwardly suffering. But where true fellowship and community exist, new insight emerges. True fellowship in a youth group frequently causes students to remark, "I thought I was the only one who felt that way." Students suffering from a poor self-image are amazed to realize that even the people who appear to "have it all together" frequently admit feelings of failure and loneliness. Real fellowship occurs when individuals grow and mature because of a group's empathy and encouragement.

The good news is: With the proper tools and the proper strategy, a group *can* be built! Dreams *can* become reality. But many times, we as youth leaders have a fatalistic attitude and overlook the tools and strategy. "Community will either develop on its own or it won't and there's not much I can do about it." *Untrue!* Getting people to truly care for one another is a process that can be taught and built into a group. Most people are not naturally vulnerable, caring and empathetic. Most people don't find it easy to share honestly with others. They need an example and some help.

One of the keys to building community in a youth group is to create an atmosphere where the youth are "forced" by the situation to share openly and to grow. This is called an active learning environment. The students can't vegetate or check out. The experience itself forces them to be involved.

As students are immersed in this atmosphere, openness and sharing begin to emerge. In addition, learning accelerates. When a group engages in an active learning environment, interest and retention are enhanced. When a high school girl successfully falls backward into the outstretched arms of her peers (page 53), she can begin to visualize what it means to trust God and trust the group. When a high school guy is bombarded with five minutes of compliments (page 89), he begins to realize the full potential God created within him: that he is lovable, acceptable and capable, and that the group has recognized this in him. He trusts the group more and an atmosphere has been created where affirmations are encouraged. Learning begins to take place from within—discovery learning—as opposed to the force-feeding approach so commonly used. The results with discovery learning are staggering. People previously bored with the church are suddenly eager to meet with their friends and grow in Christ. The dream begins to become a reality.

THE FIVE STEPS

A specific process must take place in the life of any group to bring about this type of fellowship and openness. Before an individual can share his or her struggles and begin to overcome them, he or she must trust the other members of the group. This development of trust and commitment progresses at varying speeds for different people but *all* individuals go through the five basic steps outlined below.

Step One: Bond Building

The first step in building community is to break down the cliques and barriers that exist, and to establish a trust relationship among the students. This is accomplished by giving the group members some problem-solving tasks which require them to work side by side with others in the group. As they discuss solutions and physically help one another accomplish the goal, bonds are built between people of diverse backgrounds. Cooperation is the main goal. As the students' input is accepted and welcomed by others, they begin to identify themselves as being part of the group—part of the team. Athletic teams exemplify this level of group building. Sports require only low-level sharing and vulnerability, but major emphasis is placed on teamwork and cooperation. The 23 bond building exercises presented in this book are unique in that they are short, largely noncompetitive and set in an active learning environment. They focus on group interaction and make group building easily observable.

Step Two: Opening Up

When an individual can share non-threatening areas of his or her life, an exciting step in group building has taken place. People like to talk about themselves. If a person perceives that others are genuinely interested in him or her, then telling one's peers about oneself provides an opportunity for trust to develop in the group. Unfortunately, the reverse is also true. If people perceive that others don't care to listen, trust will not be built. The more empathetically a youth group listens, the more secure a person feels when sharing his or her present struggles.

The 22 opening up strategies in this book are designed to help individuals understand the benefits of sharing with one another. The exercises are generic enough so that the students can share to whatever degree they feel comfortable. Participants go away from these activities enthusiastic about the deepening friendships they are developing in their group. They realize that their personal imperfections are not unique. When students discover they are "normal," they are able to accept and deal with their problems in a much more constructive way.

Step Three: Affirming

Crucial to the growing process of a group is the act of encouraging each other through affirmation. When a guy hears his peers complimenting him, he enjoys his participation in the group much more and is more likely to share deeper feelings. When a girl is told by her friends that they appreciate her, her feelings of self-worth dramatically increase. Many reclusive students become active participants in the group when they realize that others care about them. The 18 affirming exercises offer a structured process for individuals to tell each other why they appreciate one another and what each person's strengths are. Participants leave the meeting feeling "warm and fuzzy" about the group and themselves. This feeling is especially crucial at this stage in the process of building community. After revealing their inner selves during the opening up step, students need positive feedback to reassure them that others think they are still okay before they will consider sharing further.

Step Four: Stretching

The Bible says we are to "consider it all joy" when faced with trials, because difficult situations cause growth (James 1:2-3). Everyone goes through trials; but when these tough times are experienced as a group, opportunities arise for people to truly "bear one another's burdens."

Group members facing struggles together must actively care for each other. Individuals can't merely say they love one another in a stretching experience; they have to show it by their actions. With most groups, difficult circumstances arise naturally if the group is together long enough; for example, divorce, extreme illness, division in the church, etc. However, since many youth groups are together for only a short period and because you may not want to wait for a stretching experience to surface on its own, it is necessary to program stretching experiences.

Stretching experiences reap multifaceted benefits. They create an atmosphere where people now feel comfortable to expose their imperfections to the group. For instance, before the group travels to a hospital to visit terminally ill children, the popular "jock" who appears to have his life all together might admit his apprehensions about talking one-on-one with dying kids. This admission has a profound effect on the group. When the person sees that the group still likes him and accepts him despite his "weakness," he realizes that his facade of perfection is unnecessary. And when the self-critical group members see that even seemingly perfect people have struggles, they become free to love themselves.

Suddenly, through a simple stretching experience, individuals realize that they can achieve much more as a group than they ever could as a collection of individuals. People who are strong in one area are weak in another. Group members really do need one another.

Stretching experiences also cause tremendous personal growth. Facing and overcoming programmed difficulties give students the confidence that they *can* cope with everyday problems they face. They learn that they can accomplish more than they thought possible. They believe in themselves. Finite exercises in the "laboratory" setting make problem-solving techniques easier to learn and give students a model for facing problems at home, school and work.

Chapter 5 contains 20 stretching strategies. Students are placed in new and unfamiliar territory, and thereby experience personal growth and become a group. When fatigued students reach the summit of a seemingly impossible mountain climb through the positive encouragement of friends, they realize that they can accomplish anything with Christ and his body of believers.

Stretching exercises are much more effective when the group has gone through the bond building, opening up and affirming stages. If a person has not developed genuine trust with the group members, he or she is likely to keep apprehensions bottled inside and not benefit from the experience. If a deep trust does exist, however, individuals will open up and share their needs and weaknesses with their peers. They will allow biblical "burden bearing" to happen.

The positive results from these activities are remarkable as group members bond together and grow in all areas of their lives.

Step Five: Deeper Sharing and Goal Setting

The stage has now been set for the final and most important

step: Individuals share deeply with other members of the group and set goals. The youth group becomes the setting where students can express their inner hurts, visions and struggles. At this stage, students are not condemned or laughed at for admitting that they flunked a test from the easiest teacher in the school, or that they dream of becoming a senator, or that they have a drinking problem, or that they are overjoyed to receive a minor part in the school play.

When a group member shares a problem, the rest of the group is empathetic and gives support and encouragement. The group exists to help the individual talk through possible solutions and set goals. The group holds the individual accountable while giving him or her the freedom to fail.

It is important to keep in mind that not all of a person's deep inner thoughts are appropriate to share in a group setting. Obviously, a student should be discouraged from telling the whole youth group all the vivid details of his struggles and experiences with his girlfriend. Students need to be strongly encouraged to share these struggles with you or another leader on a one-to-one basis. The degree to which a youth leader shows a caring, empathetic attitude in the group setting will determine greatly whether students will come to him or her later for private counsel.

This book contains 23 deeper sharing and goal setting strategies. The exercises are structured to make people think about where they need spiritual growth in their own lives and then to share those areas with the group.

Action

Taking a group through the five steps is essential and growth-producing, but accomplishes only the beginning of the exercises' benefits. Once the five-step process of building community is completed, participants are ready to risk themselves in sharing with their peers in a non-programmed situation. Where initially the group members were coaxed into opening up through the use of carefully planned exercises, participants now become willing to take this step on their own.

After completing the five steps, people will volunteer their needs and allow their peers to help them with their walk with Christ. Youth leaders need to provide a time and atmosphere in weekly meetings where students have an opportunity to share.

SUGGESTIONS FOR BUILDING COMMUNITY

Before we proceed, let's look at a few general suggestions on how to use these strategies effectively with our groups.

Time Frames

With each activity, we've suggested a general time frame to do the activity and discuss what's been learned. These are *suggested* time blocks. The interest and involvement of your group will determine how much time to take.

The keys to successful timing are *sensitivity* and *flexibility*. Watch your group members' involvement level and enthusiasm. To what extent is everyone involved in the activity? The more sensitive you are to your group, the better you'll be at determining the time frame for the various exercises. The more experience you have in leading these types of activities, the better you'll be at detecting the time flow.

Whatever you do, don't short-circuit the discussion questions. You may not spend a lot of time on them, but the questions do encourage students to reflect and verbalize what's gone on.

When you feel you've obtained the maximum from the strategy for your group, cut it and move on. Too long on an activity may be worse than too short. This is where flexibility is key. The exercise might take more or less than the suggested time. Be flexible and enjoy the learning experience.

Sizing the Group

The ideal size for small group sharing is seven people. Most of the activities in this book are designed for groups of five to 10 people. If your group is larger, divide into smaller groups. However, in the youth group setting, it is not necessary to keep the same small group week after week. As students experience group building with one portion of the youth group, they can transfer what they've learned to another small group as they move to more advanced strategies.

Using the Tool

This book is strictly a resource tool. Its success relies upon the integration of the exercises with more conventional forms of ministry. Utilize the exercises in this book along with other ingredients of your youth group such as singing, praying, Bible study and service projects. *All* aspects of youth ministry are crucial. Group building is important to the extent that it serves as a building block to growth: the growth of the group, and the growth of the group's ability to minister to one another and to the world.

Reading the Group

Every youth group is different. In the same way that quarterbacks are trained to "read" the opponents' defenses, we youth workers need to "read" our group and decide which exercises in this book will meet the current needs. All groups must work their way progressively through the five levels; however, the rate at which this happens will vary. Questions that will determine what you do and how fast the group progresses include: How long have group members known one another? How much interest and ability have they shown in listening to and caring for one another? Do individuals point out each other's faults in a critical manner? We need to answer questions such as these to give us an idea of where our group is in the group building process. For example, if the group members have known each other a long time, you will not stay in the bond building stage as long. Or, if you are almost through the fourth step and you notice a student feeling extremely discouraged, you can go back to an affirming exercise. Be aware of the members' needs and be flexible as you progress through the steps.

New members and friends of youth group members can enter at any level. They will see and feel the caring between the group members and will gradually enter into the sharing process. As one person in the group exhibits openness, others will feel free to become vulnerable.

Teachable Moments

Teachable moments are those special times when a student is open to discovery. He or she is ready to learn, to discover new insights, to make changes in his or her life. As a guide, a co-learner, a teacher, a pastor, a friend, we can help the students capture and profit from these moments as they relate their actions in the exercises to everyday life. The better eye we as leaders have for teachable moments, the better the discussion.

Capitalize on teachable moments during the fourth and fifth steps of building community—stretching, and deeper sharing and goal setting. Do *not* use teachable moments when you initially do bond building, opening up and affirming. At these stages, kids are just beginning to share, risk, be vulnerable and open up. It is essential that they have the chance to do so. When you initially lead the participants through the first three steps, do not jump in at opportune moments to teach the participants a lesson. Simply listen, affirm and accept them.

When the youth have gone through the first three steps—and bonds have been built and the youth have become more secure and confident in their sharing—then use teachable moments.

We need to be sensitive and careful not to use teachable moments as an opportunity to attack the participants in their weak areas. Instead, ask questions that probe. For instance, try not to say something like, "You three girls are always together and don't care about the rest of the group. When you're involved in an activity, you never listen to other people's ideas and consequently you don't always succeed." Instead, ask probing questions in an open way; for example, "Who did you participate with in this exercise?" "As you participated, did you ignore some people's ideas?" "Have you seen that happen in the group before?" "How do you feel about that?" "How would you like to see it change?" "How could change take place?"

Below are seven typical teachable moment topics that the exercises in this book frequently bring to the forefront in a group:

1. *Leadership.* Certain students frequently take leadership roles and become deaf to the opinions of their peers. Other students do the opposite; they rarely lead. Instead, they choose to follow and not contribute much to the group even when they have an idea that could solve the exercise.

2. *Cooperation.* Some students find it difficult to work with each other and instead of cooperating in an activity, they battle against one another. Noncooperation obviously slows down the completion of the task; but as the students begin to cooperate with one another through these activities, youth meetings flow much more smoothly.

3. *Resourcefulness.* Students do not always use all of the available options and resources. Like us, they are sometimes narrow-minded and may try to solve problems while "wearing blinders." In everyday life, the youth also may overlook some of the best solutions because of the limits they have placed on their thinking. Succeeding at these exercises can help them see the bigger picture and utilize greater resources.

4. *Frustration.* The longer it takes for a group to complete a task, the higher rises the frustration level. Students learn they can do more than they thought possible if they are persistent and work through their various frustration levels.

5. *Gender.* Sometimes the group is divided in the decision-making process by gender: guys versus gals. At times one sex will dominate the other and not allow them to have ownership in the solving of the problem. The exercises in this book challenge students who are overly role-conscious; for example, the "real man" or the "miss perfect."

6. *Cliques.* The cliques that form in the youth group can hamper problem solving. Cliques, divisions and factions are potent possibilities for discussions.

7. *Loners.* Some students do all they can to avoid participation. Sometimes this is the individual's fault; sometimes this is the

group's fault. More often, it's the fault of both.

Once a group has gone through the first three steps in group building (bond building, opening up, affirming), you can use teachable moments in the fourth and fifth steps. The discussion questions in these last two steps are designed to probe teachable moments. For example, to focus on the teachable moment topic of resourcefulness a question could be, "What are some of the options you could have used, but didn't?" To focus on the teachable moment topic of cooperation a question could be, "How did you feel the group members worked together to accomplish this task?"

Once your group has gone through the first three steps in group building, you also can return to the bond building activities. We have designed teachable moments and teachable moment discussion questions for each of the bond building exercises and placed these in designated boxes. These teachable moment questions take the bond building exercises one step further and cause the students to discover new insights about themselves. For example, look at Trust Fall on page 53. As you can see, the teachable moment questions in the designated box help the students reflect deeper into themselves and apply the lessons much more than the original discussion questions. That's totally appropriate. When you're doing the Trust Fall simply as an activity to build bonds between students who may not know each other well, it is best not to ask too many probing questions. The participants simply are not ready to share on a deep level. But after they've known each other, accepted and affirmed one another, they are ready to be more honest and thoughtful within the context of the group. That's where the teachable moment questions come in.

Once we become more familiar with the community building exercises in this resource, we can modify them or make up our own to better meet the needs of the group. Here are some examples of altering activities to fit your needs:

• Take one of these exercises or a favorite activity of your's and alter the time limit.

• Give some students a handicap such as a blindfold or crutches.

• Give someone an advantage. For example, if one of your students is not being listened to by the rest of the group, do a regular bond building exercise but allow only that person to talk while the rest remain quiet.

Teaching and Counseling

An active learning environment opens new avenues for teaching and counseling. When students share their feelings and struggles, they have tremendous input in the lives of one another. This sharing broadens our ministry too. In one sense, we're allowing students to learn in the most effective way possible—learning personally and through discovery. In another way, by observing carefully, we are able to discover areas where the young people are hurting. Doors suddenly open for us in teaching and counseling as we watch carefully for those "teachable moments"—events when students are most open to discovering truth.

The exercises in this book plant seeds that later can be harvested by youth leaders. For example, a student displays grief as he tells the group about his family. As he does, your empathy in the group setting allows you to probe deeper when the two of you are alone. And as he shares, he indicates a willingness to be helped.

Pursuing the Options

This book can be used *systematically* to bring about closeness in your youth group in a relatively short period of time. Several easy, ready-to-use meetings and retreats for implementing group building are listed in Chapters 7 and 8. Choose one of these options or create your own.

You also can use these exercises *sporadically* when you feel the group needs a "shot in the arm" in a certain area. Opening a midweek Bible study with a bond building exercise can set the tone for closeness. Offering an affirming exercise midway through a long winter's month of meetings can alleviate some of the backbiting and nitpicking that has been going on.

Activities in the bond building, opening up and affirming sections should be attempted first before moving on to the more in-depth stretching experiences, and deeper sharing and goal setting exercises. Nearly all of these activities could be used at any time, but the deeper-level activities will prove to be more successful once a base of trust has been established between group members.

Remembering the Keys

Now let's look at some simple keys that can aid all of us building community in our youth group.

1. *Put people before program.* Students' needs in our groups are much more important than our preplanned programs. It's crucial to plan ahead but we need to be ready to alter our programs to meet needs that arise. For example, if we plan an evening of "deeper sharing" and then a dozen new people arrive at the

meeting, we should adjust and use a few more opening up exercises. Be flexible to accommodate your group's needs.

2. *Facilitate discussion.* For these exercises, it is best to view ourselves as "facilitators" or "guides." We should direct the discussion in certain areas by asking good questions. Many of these questions are given as part of the exercises to make your job a little easier. Feel free to add other questions. Rather than lecturing, it is extremely important for us to allow individuals an opportunity to express themselves: their thoughts, perceptions, feelings. We'll gain their respect if we care enough to listen to them. We are least helpful when we hog the show.

3. *Ask perceptive questions.* We need to refrain from asking questions with obvious answers. Students will think we're treating them like children. Questions should focus on the participants' perceptions. For example: "How did you feel when you suggested the idea to your group and they didn't use it?" "What was one of the most important things you learned from that experience?"

For the opening steps in group building, focus on practical and personal viewpoints. Questions in the later steps of group building can focus on philosophical and theological perspectives. At the beginning stages of group building, the students are just starting to open up and share. At these early stages, when issues are focused on practical and personal viewpoints, the students' interest increases dramatically.

4. *Be open.* If *we* don't model vulnerability and openness to our group members, *they* won't reflect vulnerability or openness. It can be difficult as well as humbling to show our hurts and struggles, but group members have the capacity to respond with amazing grace, love and care. After you share, they will be more willing to open up and share their hurts. Personal modeling and example are absolutely crucial. *We* set the stage for openness.

5. *Know when to refer.* Chances are that few of us are trained psychologists. Most of the time, we more than adequately can minister to the vast majority of problems and struggles we encounter, but sometimes we can get in "over our head" in a counseling situation. Individuals who are suicidal, victims of child abuse, or people who suffer from other deep emotional problems probably need more professional help than we can provide. Empathizing, listening and providing direction to these people are helpful, but we need to refer them to a qualified Christian psychologist or psychiatrist if the individual is to receive adequate care.

It is important that group members feel the freedom to share their hurts with us. Exercises are included in this book that will help that to happen. The most effective way to minister to the youth is to share how God has helped you in a similar area of struggle. If you have not experienced a similar struggle, you may want to send that student to a person who has or to a professional counselor.

6. *Use the exercises with other groups.* This book is designed for youth groups. The group building strategies in an active learning environment are, however, applicable to almost every age group. For example, families with older children can benefit by doing many of the exercises around the dinner table or on family nights. Some of the stretching exercises can be planned during vacation times.

College students and young adults are facing many of life's big questions and determining who they are and what values they wish to possess. These exercises will help them in their quest for community and in working to answer crucial questions.

Leadership retreats, all-church potlucks, ministerial conferences, women's retreats, senior citizen meetings are only a few of the events that can benefit from group building. Whether it's one hour or one week, these exercises can add spice and substance to any program.

With all those suggestions in mind, let's "exercise" and look at specific strategies for building community in your youth group.

Questions for Reflection

1. What has been one of your favorite "scenes" in your time as a youth leader? least favorite?

2. At which step in the five-step process of building community do you think your group will have the greatest degree of difficulty? Why?

3. In 25 words or less, how would you describe your group?

4. Of the six keys mentioned in this chapter (see pages 26-28), which one do you think you practice more effectively? Why? On which key will you need to concentrate more? Why?

5. What's been one of the most helpful things you've learned in this chapter? Why?

CHAPTER 2:
BOND BUILDING

Scene One

"We just can't do it!" the high school senior exclaimed. "We've tried every possible solution!"

The youth leader remained silent as he watched the group attempting to climb over the "electric fence"—a 5-foot-high piece of string. The group members had been instructed that they must get over and not touch the fence if they were to escape "electrocution" and they were frustrated in their attempts to succeed.

Eventually, a ninth grade girl suggested an alternative that worked. In the discussion that followed, the high school senior commented, "I wasn't seeking the advice of younger members of the group during this exercise, yet they came up with the best answers. I need to realize that the input of people younger than myself is important."

Scene Two

Don, a sophomore who hung out with "the rough crowd" at school, sat off to the side of the group as the youth meeting was about to begin. His actions and expressions illustrated his discomfort at being in the group with "upper-class jocks." When the meeting started, he immediately found himself in the middle of a bond building exercise. Don was compelled to interact and cooperate with those he disliked. Through the exercise he began to feel more comfortable and included. He was less of an outsider and he liked that feeling.

Bond building strategies are problem-solving tasks that force students to work together in an atmosphere that builds cohesiveness. As students work side by side and are encouraged to learn insights about themselves in a non-threatening environment, unity begins to develop within the group. These fun, short, shared experiences break down initial barriers which exist between students. Bonds are built.

Bond building exercises are effective because they place people in situations that force them to overcome physical and emotional barriers. Each person becomes a participant in the fulfillment of the task. As the participants struggle together toward the solution of the exercise, the shyer, quieter students find they have as much to contribute to the group's success as do their more outgoing peers. Bond building activities are unique in that they build a student's self-esteem as he or she overcomes what was first thought impossible. The exercises help individuals see their strengths as well as those of their fellow group members. The strategies are catalysts for deeper sharing; they encourage people to communicate with one another.

Bond building strategies are unique in that most learning takes place in the exercises themselves rather than in the discussion that follows. Students discover new insights about themselves and the group as they participate. The key to maximum retention of what has been learned in the bond building exercise is "verbalization." When students discuss with their peers the things they have learned, insights are clarified and better remembered. In addition, students hear that others have learned from the exercise and even more insights emerge.

How to Use the Bond Building Exercises

1. *Carefully select a bond building exercise.* In advance, carefully read the descriptions, instructions and questions for best results.

2. *Be a silent participant.* The key purpose of bond building games is group interaction. More learning takes place when the leader offers hints or suggestions, but steps out of the decision-making process. (The group members usually take the leader's advice, but aren't forced to reach decisions on their own.) Do not succumb to the temptation to give students the "right" or "best" answer. In most cases, it's best for leaders to silently participate in the exercise. Youth gain a new respect for leaders when the students are allowed to tell the leaders what to do!

3. *Be extremely safety conscious.* The exercises in this chapter are safe but many of them require "spotters"—people who stand

to the side and prevent injuries if a participant slips and falls.

4. *Use small groups.* Divide into smaller groups if your entire youth group is larger than the recommended size for the exercise.

5. *Offer clear instructions.* Give the group clear and specific rules and instructions for the task. Take extra time if necessary. The set-up is very important to success.

6. *Spend little or no time in discussing mistakes.* During the discussion, focus on the ultimate success the participants had as they worked together to solve a problem and achieve the goals of the exercise.

7. *Wait for answers.* When you ask a question, give time for a response. Don't be afraid of silence. When students get uncomfortable enough with the silence, they will answer. If you answer your own question once, students will wait for you to answer the next time. By waiting, you show that you genuinely value the students' opinions and they more readily will enter into discussion and benefit from it. After asking a question, try mentally counting to 15 before saying anything.

8. *Focus on the students' personal experiences and feelings.* Once personal feelings are discussed, the philosophical and theological implications of the exercise can come alive. To abbreviate the process and first concentrate on philosophical concepts is to miss the point of bond building.

9. *Be sure everyone gets an opportunity to talk.* If the group seems reluctant to share or if a few individuals dominate the conversation, go around the circle and ask each person to respond with his or her feelings; for example, "How did you feel, Janet, as you tried to help the group get over the fence?" Going around the circle and asking feeling questions is a fairly non-threatening method to facilitate discussion.

10. *Refrain from giving advice.* Students need adults who will listen; they reject most pat answers. We minister and show we care by empathetically listening. Indeed, as group members interact and share with each other, they often come up with the same or better solutions than we may have suggested.

11. *Replay the activities.* After you have taken your students through the first three steps in group building, you can come back to the bond building exercises. The students will be ready to share more deeply. When you replay the activities, use the teachable moment discussion questions in the designated boxes.

Think of these tips on how to use these exercises as you begin the process of building community in your youth group.

ALL TIED UP

Time: 25 minutes.
Materials: one 18-inch piece of cord per participant.
Group Size: any number.

Description

1. Have the students form a circle. Use the 18-inch pieces of cord to tie each person's wrists to the wrists of the persons standing on either side.

2. Play Simon Says. Suggested activities are: Touch your toes, do jumping jacks, put your hand on your neighbor's head, clap your hands, do two push-ups, etc.

Discussion

1. What do you see as the purpose of this exercise?
2. What was the most difficult aspect?
3. What did you learn from it?

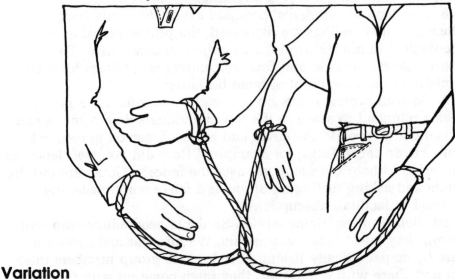

Variation

Divide the group into pairs and give each person a 3-foot cord. Have one person in each pair tie the ends of his or her cord to his or her wrists. Have the other person in the pair loop his or her cord through the partner's cord and then tie the ends to his or her wrists. The two partners are now connected.

Ask the pairs to try to disentangle without untying the cord. It is possible. Instruct the successful participants not to help those who are still trying to disentangle. (Note: If after one year you are not able to come up with a solution, write to Denny Rydberg, 15208 NE 110th Pl., Redmond, WA 98052. He will send you the solution!)

Teachable Moment

This exercise illustrates dependence on a partner, the importance of carefully listening to instructions, and the effect of one person in the body of Christ. The variation stresses the importance of patience, creative thinking, perseverance and observation.

Discussion

1. What was the most frustrating part of this exercise for you? How did you deal with your frustration?

2. What are some things that frustrate you in life? How have you learned to deal with them?

3. What did you learn from this exercise that you can apply to handling frustrations in your daily life?

4. In the variation of this activity, who was the prime problem solver in your pair?

5. Who are some of the prime problem solvers in your life?

6. To whom do you serve as chief problem solver? How? How well do you like that role? Why?

BLIND ALPHABET

Time: 15 minutes.
Materials: one blindfold for each participant, one 10-foot cord.
Group Size: six to 13.

Description

1. Give the group members the long piece of cord. Ask them to grasp the cord with both hands.

2. Blindfold all of the students.

3. Tell the group a letter of the alphabet to create with the cord.

4. Have the group members decide when they have completed the task. (Don't tell them.)

5. Repeat the exercise several times, having the group create different letters or shapes.

Discussion

1. In what ways did this task at first seem unsolvable?

2. How did you overcome your visual handicap?

3. Who emerged as leaders the different times you created letters?

Variation

If your youth group has members whose input is seldom given

or who are consistently ignored, repeat the exercise allowing one or two of these members to take off their blindfolds. If for any other reason you would like to highlight a certain student's leadership, let that person be the only one without a blindfold.

Teachable Moment

In this exercise, the youth gain greater appreciation for their sight and a better understanding of the blind. The following important topics arise: teamwork under difficult conditions, compensation for one handicap with group strengths, communication, group leadership dynamics.

Discussion

1. If you *had* to be handicapped, which of the following would you choose? Deafness, blindness, loss of a leg or paralysis. Why?

2. What would be the worse thing for you about having this handicap?

3. How could this handicap be a blessing in your life?

4. Do you know a person who is physically handicapped? What have you learned from that person?

BLIND LINE UP

Time: 15 minutes.
Materials: none.
Group Size: six to 15.

Description

1. Have the participants close their eyes while the instructions are given.

2. Tell the group members to line up—without speaking or looking—according to height. Do not tell them which end of the line is the short or tall end. Have the group members decide when they have completed the task. (Don't tell them.)

3. Repeat the exercise several times, having the youth line up according to shoe size or the month in which they were born. You also can have them divide into groups according to the color of their eyes.

4. Remember to have a "spotter" to keep people from running into the walls or getting hurt.

Discussion

1. What was the most difficult part of this exercise for you?

2. Why was it difficult to get started with the exercise?

3. What did this bond building activity teach you about communication?

4. How did you benefit from this exercise?

Teachable Moment

This activity focuses on greater appreciation for the gifts of sight and speech, the importance of nonverbal communication, the importance of team—work under difficult conditions, and insight into how group leadership works under difficult conditions.

Discussion

1. What did you learn about communication from this exercise?

2. How would you evaluate your skills as a communicator in everyday life? How could you improve?

3. What did you learn from this exercise that could help you better communicate to others?

CLAUSTROPHOBIA LUNCH

Time: 35 minutes.

Materials: a 50-foot piece of cord and enough food to feed the entire group. The lunch should be one requiring some preparation by the students during the activity; for example, mix the juice, make the peanut butter and jelly sandwiches, cut the cake, etc. You also will need paper plates, cups, napkins and utensils to prepare the food.

Group Size: any number.

Description

1. Ask the group members to show how little space they can jam together in while sitting on the floor.

2. As soon as they've crammed together, put the cord on the floor closely around the perimeter of the group.

3. Give the students the following instructions:

• Everyone must help prepare lunch.

• Everyone must stay within the confines of the cord until all people are finished eating lunch.

• No one can communicate verbally or nonverbally for the first 10 minutes.

4. Distribute the ingredients for lunch and have the participants prepare and eat the food.

Discussion

1. Describe your experiences.

2. Why do you think we did this exercise?
3. What was difficult?
4. What did you learn from this experience?

Teachable Moment

Students have to be aware of the needs of the people around them so that all group members are fed. The youth learn to be patient with their peers during difficult times. Sitting close to several people in silence is difficult and can be trying for some students.

Discussion

1. How did you feel sitting jammed together waiting for the food to come?
2. Did any of you attempt to (or want to) crawl over people to get the food? Did some of you get impatient waiting for the slower eaters to finish eating? What do these actions and attitudes teach you about yourself?
3. Would you have had enough to eat if you hadn't been given permission to talk after the first 10 minutes? How does this make you feel?
4. How comfortable are you being silent around others? Explain.

CLIMBING THE WALLS

Time: 15 minutes.
Materials: tape or chalk and a wall.
Group Size: six to 15.

Description

1. Give the group some tape or chalk (depending upon the type of wall you are using).
2. Instruct the youth about the importance of using "spotters" to soften the landing if someone takes a tumble. Tell them that they only can use the wall and others in the group for support. Give the group members eight minutes to see how high a mark they can make on the wall. (For safety's sake, the group should not be allowed to get more than three people in height.)

Discussion

1. What part did you play in this exercise?
2. What did you learn from this exercise?
3. What surprised you during this experience?

Teachable Moment

During this exercise, there is a potential for domination by the more athletic students. Important topics are: learning through planning as well as trial and error, greater appreciation for the spotter who doesn't necessarily seem essential to a project.

Discussion

1. Did you feel more like a participant or an observer in this exercise? Why? How did that make you feel?
2. Who do you think may have felt left out? Why?
3. How did you seek to include everyone in this activity?
4. Describe some experiences from school when you or someone you know was deliberately left out. How do you suppose God feels about that? What would he want you to do in those kinds of situations?

ELECTRIC FENCE

Time: 30 minutes.
Materials: 15-foot piece of string.
Group Size: six to 12.

Description

1. Tie the string 5 feet off the ground between two objects that are at least 10 feet apart.
2. Tell the students that their goal is to get the whole group over the string without touching it. It is illegal to use the objects the string is tied to for support. Have the group members visualize an "electric field" extending from the string to the ground. If they touch the string or cross beneath it they become "electrocuted." The "shocked" individual must try again.
3. To prevent twisted ankles, use "spotters," especially for the first few people over the fence. Don't allow the group or individuals to make uncontrolled leaps over the fence. They must be caught.
4. To make the exercise more difficult, don't allow the participants to talk.

Discussion

1. What do you see as the purpose of this exercise?
2. What were some examples of "teamwork" you observed during this activity?

3. What else did you learn?

Variations

1. Increase the number of participants. This exercise has been done with over 50 people.

2. Instead of string, use a 5-inch-by-10-foot pole. Raise the fence 12 inches.

Teachable Moment

In this exercise, there is a potential for domination by the more athletic students. This activity stresses teamwork and cooperation—everyone is important.

Discussion

1. What was your part in getting the group over the fence?

2. How did you feel about what you contributed?

3. Which of the following roles best describes you? Mr. or Ms. Muscle, Brains, Yell Leader, Health and Safety Instructor, Hero, Entertainer or Referee.

4. What criteria determined your role? Why did you portray this role in this exercise?

5. What is important about each of the roles listed in the third question?

6. What would have happened if you hadn't made your contribution?

7. What have you learned from this discussion?

8. Relate what you learned to Romans 12:3-8.

FARMER'S RIDDLE

Time: 20 minutes.
Materials: none.
Group Size: eight.

Description

1. Designate a place in the room to be a river. Appoint different students to be two chickens, two foxes, two bags of grain and two farmers. Each student must take on the characteristics of his or her new identity; for example, the chickens can only cluck, the bags of grain can only lay around until the farmers move them, etc.

2. The farmers have to physically carry the chickens, foxes and bags of grain across the river. The farmers must travel together.

3. The foxes cannot be unsupervised with the chickens or they will eat them; the chickens cannot be left unattended with the

grain or they will eat it.

Discussion

    1. What was your biggest frustration in this exercise?
    2. How did the group eventually solve the problem?
    3. What else did you learn?

Teachable Moment

    In this exercise the students: learn the importance of advance planning, gain new insights into problem solving, and deal with frustration.

Discussion

    1. Who were the key players in solving the problem? What did you learn from them?
    2. How do you usually attempt to solve problems in your life?
    3. What is one of the greatest problems you're facing right now in your life? How do you think the group can help you solve that problem?

GUMDROP TOWER

Time: 15 minutes.
Materials: one bag of gumdrops, one box of wooden matches and one bag of uncooked spaghetti noodles.
Group Size: two to four.

Description

    1. Give the group members the gumdrops, matches and noodles. Tell them they have 10 minutes to build a tower as high as possible. The tower must be able to stand without being held up.
    2. To make the exercise more difficult, don't allow the students to talk to one another.

Discussion

    1. How did the group work together?
    2. What frustrated you in this exercise?
    3. What did you learn?

Teachable Moment

    The tendency with this exercise is for groups to begin quickly to build without creating a plan of action. Sometimes the quiet individual may emerge with a workable solution after the more vocal participants have tried several unsuccessful methods.

Discussion

    1. How many different ideas did you consider in making your tower?
    2. What were the members' roles in building the tower?
    3. How did you feel about your role?
    4. In what ways did you function well as a group?
    5. How could you have improved your interaction as a group?

HUMAN HOOP SHOOT

Time: 35 minutes.
Materials: 10-foot-high basketball hoop without a net.
Group Size: six to 15.

Description

    1. Tell the group members that they must put half of the participants through a 10-foot basketball hoop.
    2. Instruct the group members about the need for safety. Be sure several youth are used as "spotters."
    3. Care must be given to insure against damage to the rim and backboard.

Discussion

    1. In what ways were *all* of the group members needed to accomplish this task?
    2. How does this exercise relate to the concept of the "body of Christ"?

Teachable Moment

    This activity illustrates the need for supporting one another and the importance of creativity and hard work in solving a problem.

Discussion

1. How would you characterize the roles each person played in the exercise (e.g., Tom was a "lifter," Jack was a "spotter," Karen was a "climber," etc.)?

2. What role did you play? Is this typical of the role you usually play in life? Why?

3. What role do you play in your youth group? Do you like this role? Why?

4. Do you feel appreciated by others in the group? How?

5. What's one of the most important truths you've learned from Human Hoop Shoot?

KNOTS

Time: 15 minutes.
Materials: none.
Group Size: six to 15.

Description

1. Ask the group members to form a circle.

2. Have each person stretch his or her right hand into the center of the circle and grab any hand (except for the persons' next to him or her).

3. Have the participants repeat this process with the left hands. Make sure that no one is holding two hands of the same individual.

4. Once the group members are in this knot, tell them to untangle—without letting go of hands. It is legal to readjust a grip if an arm gets twisted, but the placement of that grip within the knot must remain the same.

5. To make the exercise more difficult, untangle without talking.

Note: Knots is excellent at breaking down barriers between people who don't know each other well. It serves as a great introduction to bond building exercises for those who previously have not played them.

Discussion

1. What was the purpose of this exercise?
2. What problems did you have getting untangled?
3. What was your level of participation?
4. Who solved the problem?
5. What did you learn from this exercise?

Variations

1. If a group has more than 10 people in one circle, do the first three steps to connect all participants. Have one couple drop their grasp from each other. Untangle to form a line.

2. Have the group make a circle facing inward. Ask the youth to cross their arms and join hands with the people next to them. Without letting go, the group members must get their arms un-crossed and return to a circle facing inward.

Teachable Moment

This activity stresses teamwork and creativity in solving a problem.

Discussion

1. How well did the group cooperate to accomplish the task?
2. What suggestions do you have to improve the amount of teamwork?
3. Did the group try creating new ways to untangle?
4. How does this activity relate to events in your own life?

LAP SIT

Time: 15 minutes.
Materials: none.
Group Size: 10 to 100.

Description

1. Ask all participants to stand in a circle. Ask each person to turn clockwise and get close to the back of the person in front of him or her. Make sure the circle is tight!

2. All together, have everyone gently sit down on the lap of the person behind him or her. If unsuccessful the first time, get closer together and try again.

Discussion

1. What is the purpose of this activity?
2. What factors determined whether you could maintain a sitting position in the circle? (For example, participation from everyone.)
3. What did you learn?

Variations

1. While in the lap-sit position, try walking—moving the circle

merry-go-round style.
2. While in the lap-sit position, try playing catch with a ball.

Teachable Moment

This activity focuses on the importance of every member's participation for success. Students learn to trust each other and have faith in the outcome.

Discussion

1. How well do you think the group worked together in successfully accomplishing this exercise?
2. What grade would you give the group members for the way they work together in everyday life? Explain.
3. How would you characterize your participation with your group? Explain the reasons for your level of participation.

LINE UP ON A LOG

Time: 15 minutes.
Materials: a log or beam long enough to allow the whole group to stand on it.
Group Size: six to 15.

Description

1. Begin by telling everyone to get on the log.
2. Tell the group members to line up according to height without talking or stepping off the log. Do not tell them which end of the log is the short or tall end.
3. Repeat the exercise several times, having the youth line up according to middle initial or month in which they were born.
4. Remember to have a "spotter."
5. If a person falls off the log, the group must start over.

Discussion

1. What ways of moving around one another proved most successful?
2. How did holding onto one another make the exercise easier?
3. What else did you learn from this exercise?

Teachable Moment

The students learn the importance of patience when working closely together in a tight situation.

Discussion
1. What did you like about this activity?
2. Who seemed to provide the most leadership? How?
3. Was there anyone who frustrated you as you tried to solve this problem? How? How did you express this frustration?
4. Who are some of the people you really need to cooperate with this week? Explain. How can the group help you in this area?

MURDER MYSTERY

Time: 30 minutes.
Materials: 15 envelopes—each containing one of the clues listed in step 3, one copy of the handout (see step 1) for each student.
Group Size: five to seven.

Description
1. Distribute the following handout of suspects, weapons and places:

Suspects	Weapons	Places
Fred Frogface	Lawn mower	Bunker Hill
Martha Mooselips	Plunger	Camp David
Barry Blowchips	Vacuum cleaner	The World Trade Center
Rhonda Rhinolegs	Microwave oven	Disneyland
Arnold Armpit	Tuba	The San Diego Zoo
Teresa Toejam		The Washington Monument

2. Read the following statement to the group:
"Your goal is to find out who killed Bobby Buffalobreath, what weapon was used, and where the murder occurred. The murder was done single-handedly by one of the six suspects you have listed before you. The murderer used one of those weapons at one of those locations. Each of your group members will be given two or three envelopes which contain clues. Here are the rules:
• You may read your clues *aloud* to the group as often as you wish, but you may *not* at any time let other group members see your clues.
• You may *not* write down the clues you hear being read to you.
• You may *not* use a writing utensil for any purpose at all.
• You will be timed to see how fast you are able to obtain the correct answers."
Reread the rules and ask the students if they have any questions.

3. After answering the participants' questions, distribute the envelopes so that each student has two or three of the following clues:
- Fred Frogface did *not* do it.
- The vacuum cleaner was the only weapon at the San Diego Zoo.
- *If* the murder weapon was a tuba, Barry Blowchips did it.
- Fred Frogface had the only plunger.
- The murder weapon was *not* the vacuum cleaner.
- *If* the murder occurred at the Washington Monument, Martha Mooselips did it.
- The plunger was the only weapon at Disneyland.
- Arnold Armpit was with Teresa Toejam when the murder occurred.
- The tuba was the only weapon at Bunker Hill.
- Rhonda Rhinolegs was the only suspect at the San Diego Zoo.
- The murder did not occur at the World Trade Center.
- The only lawn mower was at Camp David.
- Teresa Toejam was at Bunker Hill when the murder occurred.
- The murder did *not* occur at Camp David.
- There was only one suspect at the murder site.

4. Instruct the youth to begin and time them.

5. The correct answer is: *Martha Mooselips* killed Bobby with a *microwave oven* at the *Washington Monument*.

Discussion

1. What is this exercise designed to teach the group?

2. List some examples of group cooperation you observed while doing this exercise.

3. What did you learn from this activity?

Teachable Moment

This exercise causes the participants to listen to one another. This exercise also challenges the students' concentration and retention of facts. They have to work closely together in solving a problem which has only one very specific solution.

Discussion

1. What frustrations did you have during this exercise?

2. How did you overcome your frustrations and complete the task?

3. In what ways do you feel that the group worked well together?

4. In what ways do you feel the group didn't work well

together?

5. What else did you learn from this exercise?

NUCLEAR HOLOCAUST

Time: 30 minutes.
Materials: separate slips of paper with different descriptions of injuries (see step 2), two to three blindfolds.
Group Size: six to eight.

Description

1. Explain to the students that a nuclear explosion has just occurred. They are all injured and will have to travel—either alone or with someone—to the "hospital" (a designated spot 50 to 75 feet from the victims).

2. Give each person a piece of paper which describes his or her injury. When a person reads his or her injury, he or she must immediately assume that position; for example, an unconscious victim is unable to share with the group that he is unconscious, etc. Injuries for a group of six can include: unconscious, mute, blind and mute, paralyzed and blind, mute and can't use left leg, has no use of arms or legs.

If the group is larger, duplicate some of the listed injuries for the additional participants.

3. The game is most successful if the outgoing students receive the more debilitating injuries, and the shy participants receive the minor ailments.

4. One of the group leaders should be an observer—to prevent possible injury (the blind leading the blind, etc.).

Discussion

1. How did you get to the hospital?
2. What people did you observe helping others?
3. What did you learn from this exercise?

Teachable Moment

Nuclear Holocaust focuses students on the concept of the "body of Christ" and how different people have different talents, but all are needed to make the "body" function properly.

Discussion

1. How did you feel in the role you were assigned?
2. Did you work as a group, or was it "each man for himself"?

3. Which of the given roles would have been the most difficult for you to assume? Explain.

4. What did you learn about yourself during this exercise?

5. What did you learn about "community"?

6. How does Ecclesiastes 4:9-12 relate to this bond building exercise?

POINTS OF CONTACT

Time: 15 minutes.
Materials: a soft, flat area.
Group Size: six to 13.

Description

1. Mark off start and finish lines at least 10 yards apart.

2. Multiply the number of participants in the group by 3/5 and round up to the nearest whole number. This is the number of "points of contact" the group is allowed. For example: nine participants x 3/5 = 27/5 = 5 2/5 rounded up to six points of contact.

3. The group must move as a connected unit across the 10 yards with only the designated number of "points of contact" touching the ground. Each hand or foot is considered a point of contact. If a person switches from one leg to the other while traveling the 10 yards, he or she is using two points of contact. If more than the allotted points are used, the group must start over.

4. Members of the group must be connected in some way to each other (for example, hook elbows) and they must move as a unit across the 10 yards. If they separate while crossing, they must start over.

5. At least two "spotters" are necessary to guard from injury anyone who starts to fall.

Discussion

1. What do you see as the purpose for doing this exercise?

2. How did the group accomplish this purpose?

3. What was your role in the exercise?

4. What did you learn?

Teachable Moment

Points of Contact tends to cause initial frustration among students because of the seeming impossibility of the task. The participants *do* learn about problem solving and persistence from this exercise. Some students who stand back and watch at first are often the first ones to come up with the solution that works.

Discussion

1. What were your dominant feelings during this exercise? Explain.
2. What did you contribute to the solving of the problem?
3. Did you have any ideas which you chose not to share with the group? Why?
4. What finally worked for the group?
5. What did you learn from this exercise?

RADIOACTIVE SWAMP

Time: 25 minutes.
Materials: three pieces of cardboard or paper per group. Make each piece of cardboard approximately the size of a person's foot.
Group Size: four to five per group.

Description

1. Mark off your "swamp" with start and finish lines at least 10 yards apart.
2. Divide into groups of four to five. Designate a light person in each group to have paralyzed legs. Tell the groups that they must attempt to get all of their members across the radioactive swamp without getting contaminated.
3. Give each group three pieces of cardboard which act as insulators from the chemicals.
4. Each participant must get across the swamp without touching the deadly chemicals (the ground). Only one foot can be placed on each insulator at one time. Only the insulators protect the individuals from the chemicals.
5. If a person touches the ground with a body part, he or she cannot use that part for the rest of the exercise. If a person's whole body touches the ground, he or she must start over.
6. The "insulating blocks" may not be thrown across the swamp. Someone must bring them back each time.
7. The insulating blocks may not be slid. They must be picked up and placed where the participant wants them.

Discussion

1. In what ways did you work together as a group to accomplish this exercise?
2. Who sacrificed a great deal for the success of the group?

3. How did the presence of the "paralyzed" person in the group affect the way you went about solving the problem?

4. How did the "paralyzed" person feel throughout this exercise?

5. What else did you learn from this exercise?

Teachable Moment

In this exercise, the students learn the importance of advance planning, new insights into problem solving, dealing with frustration and perseverance.

Discussion

1. What is one thing you learned about problem solving that you can apply to solving the problems in your own life?

2. Who are some of the "paralyzed" people in your life? How can you help them?

3. In what ways, if at all, do you feel paralyzed?

4. Who are the people who help "carry" you?

SAND CASTLES

Time: 35 minutes.

Materials: a few toy shovels, buckets of various sizes, sandy area or sand box.

Group Size: four to seven.

Description

1. If you live near a beach or a sandy area, this adaptation of building sand castles is extremely easy and fun. If you don't live near a sandy area, borrow a sand box from a preschool.

2. Tell the group members that they will have 30 minutes to create a work of art out of sand.

3. Inform the youth that they must all work on the *same* piece of art.

Discussion

1. How did you decide what art object to create?

2. Give examples of cooperation you observed between group members.

Variation

Form pairs and tie their wrists together. Have each pair create a work of art.

Teachable Moment

Building sand castles as a group requires numerous decisions, none of which are "right" or "wrong." Thus, group members must brainstorm ideas and "give and take" considerably if the task is to be accomplished.

Discussion

1. What frustrations did you encounter during the exercise?
2. Who emerged as the leader?
3. Whose opinion should the group members have listened to more than they did?

SENSES

Time: 40 minutes.
Materials: one blindfold, one good pair of earplugs and one scarf for every four people. Plan activities such as table games or preparing a pizza dinner.
Group Size: six to 15.

Description

1. Deprive each participant of one of the following: sight (blind-fold him or her), hearing (use ear-plugs—instruct the other students to communicate through whispering if earplugs are not effective enough), touch (tie the person's hands behind his or her back with the scarf), voice (do not allow the person to talk).
2. Do 30 minutes of activities such as table games or preparation of a pizza dinner.

Discussion

1. How did the handicap affect you during this exercise?
2. What did you learn about teamwork from this exercise?

Teachable Moment

Students will need to depend upon one another (some more than others). The degree of the participants' response to the needs of others will be enlightening.

Discussion

1. How did being deprived of a body sense affect you?
2. How did you compensate for your handicap?
3. What did you do to help the other handicapped people?
4. Do you think one part of your body is more important than the rest?
5. Read 1 Corinthians 12:12-27. How did this exercise relate to these verses?
6. Does being deprived of one member of this youth group affect you?
7. Do you think different members of the body of Christ are more important than others? Explain.
8. What did you learn from this exercise?

SERVANT'S LUNCH

Time: 30 minutes.
Materials: enough food for the entire group. This lunch will be made by the participants *during* the activity. Bring food such as ham, cheese, mayonnaise, mustard, bread, potato chips and juice. You also will need napkins, paper plates, cups and utensils to prepare the food.
Group Size: any number.

Description

1. Set out the food and other supplies.
2. Instruct the group members that during lunch no person can prepare or ask for food for himself or herself.
3. Individuals *can* feed themselves if someone else prepares it for them.
4. Rules must be strictly enforced for this activity to be successful.
5. Proceed with the activity.

Discussion

1. How did you like being fed (or served)?
2. In what ways was it hard to think of someone else's needs?
3. Are any of you still hungry? If so, why didn't you eat until you were full?
4. What do you *think* you were supposed to learn from this activity?
5. What did you learn?

Variation

Divide the group into pairs. Instruct the participants to prepare food and feed it to their partner. They may not feed, prepare or ask for food for themselves.

Teachable Moment

In this exercise, the students gain personal insights into how selfish people can be with their food. They overcome negative attitudes about letting others serve.

Discussion

1. Do you feel more comfortable in everyday life serving or being served? Why?

2. Who do you think God is calling you to serve this week? Explain.

3. Who do you need to let serve you? Why is this important?

4. What problems, if any, do you have with food? How are you dealing with those problems?

STAND UP

Time: 20 minutes.
Materials: none.
Group Size: any number.

Description

1. Divide the group into pairs.

2. Have the partners sit on the floor, back-to-back.

3. Ask the partners to link arms together and try to stand up (keeping arms interlocked at all times).

4. After a pair has succeeded, have them get together with another pair, sit down, link arms and stand up.

5. Keep combining groups until everyone is in one large group and can stand up.

Discussion

1. What was the deciding factor in being able to stand up? (For example, 100 percent commitment.)

2. How is this exercise similar to the relationships we have with others?

3. What happened as you added more people? Why?

4. How is this concept similar to relationships in groups?

5. What else did you learn?

Teachable Moment

The students learn the need to be committed 100 percent to the group.

Discussion

1. How difficult is it for you to commit to something?
2. What determines your commitment level to a group?
3. How good are you at staying committed?
4. What are some things you wish you had been more committed to? Why?
5. At present, what are your three greatest commitments?

TRUST FALL

Time: 20 minutes.
Materials: chair or platform that is 4 to 6 feet high.
Group Size: nine to 13.

Description

1. Ask the students to remove their watches and glasses. Have the group form two lines facing one another.
2. Instruct the students to stretch their arms out in front of them, palms upward, in a position to catch a falling person. Do not have them lock arms with the people across from them. Instead, have them alternate arms with those standing opposite them.
3. Encourage all individuals to participate in this activity, yet do not force them. The first person climbs up on a chair or platform that is 4 to 6 feet high and falls backward into the group.
4. With a few of the people, instead of letting them down after catching them, lift them up above your heads and carry them around. You also can have the group count to three, carefully toss the individual a couple of feet in the air and then catch him or her.

By challenging the participants' fear of height, this exercise forces them to physically put their trust in the group.

Discussion

1. What did it feel like to fall into your group members' arms?
2. What did you learn from this experience?

Teachable Moment

This exercise helps the students realize the difficulty and

necessity of trusting others.

Discussion

1. Which of you had difficulty convincing yourself to participate in this activity? Explain.

2. After the group caught you, how were your fears diminished? How difficult would it have been to fall a second time?

3. How did you feel being a "catcher" of the falling person? What was it like being responsible for another person's physical well-being?

4. How are you responsible for others in everyday life?

5. Which is more difficult for you—trusting someone with your physical body or trusting someone with your inner thoughts and feelings? Explain.

6. What have you learned about trust through this exercise?

TRUST WALK

Time: 25 minutes.
Materials: one blindfold for every two people.
Group Size: any number.

Description

1. Divide the students into pairs.

2. One student in each pair puts on a blindfold.

3. Instruct the sighted person to take his or her partner on a walk. This is most successfully done outdoors. The sighted people should hold hands with their partners and have them walk and jog over uneven ground and go up and down stairs.

4. A portion of the walk should be done without talking.

5. Partners then switch the blindfold to the sighted person.
Caution the students to use common sense. For example, jumping from a height as short as 2 feet could easily cause injury.

Discussion

1. Describe your walk.

2. Which was easier for you—being blindfolded or leading the blind?

3. What did you learn from this exercise?

Teachable Moment

In the Trust Walk, two issues stand out consistently: appreciation of the gift of sight, and the difficulty of trusting God and friends.

Discussion

1. How did it feel to be completely dependent upon someone?
2. What were you afraid of?
3. Discuss this acrostic of fear:
   False
   Evidence
   Appearing
   Real
4. Is it more difficult to trust someone with your physical well-being or with your thoughts and feelings? Why?
5. In your everyday life, are most people trustworthy? Who do you know that is trustworthy? Why do you think these people are trustworthy if most people aren't?
6. How have people violated your trust? Why do you think they have done that?
7. While you were the sighted person in this exercise, what was it like having someone completely dependent upon you?
8. How trustworthy are you with people's thoughts and feelings? How can you become more trustworthy?
9. How can you help others to become more trustworthy? For example, by modeling trustworthy behavior, taking personal risks of self-disclosure, responding to the other person with acceptance and support.

TUBES

Time: 15 minutes.
Materials: one inner tube for every three people.
Group Size: six to nine.

Description

1. Establish start and finish lines 10 yards apart.
2. Give one inner tube to every three people.
3. Tell the groups that they must use the tubes to travel together across the 10 yards, without stepping on the ground. The tubes may only go across the 10 yards once.
4. To make this exercise more difficult, don't let the participants talk.

Discussion

1. Was there a "key" to making this exercise work?

2. How did the group have to work together to accomplish the task?

3. What was each person's role in accomplishing the task of getting across?

4. What else did you learn from this exercise?

Teachable Moment

This exercise stresses total group participation and cooperation.

Discussion

1. How did you feel about participating in this exercise? Why?

2. When can you remember not wanting to participate in something but doing it anyway?

3. Was it a positive or negative experience for you? Why?

CHAPTER 3:
OPENING UP

Students love to talk about themselves *when they feel comfortable and accepted.*

When a group cares enough to listen intently to what every individual has to say, the group comes alive! A sense of unity surfaces; friendships develop; barriers break down.

For an individual, opening up also has some advantages. Ideas are expressed, accepted and confidence builds. Opening up increases awareness and understanding. The more often a person shares, he or she discovers new insights about God, self, life and others.

Openness and vulnerability are important to a group and to the individuals in the group. But for a youth group to open up, two critical steps must be taken. The first step is *risking*, which primarily involves the individual. The second step is *responding*, which primarily involves the group as a whole. In the first step, students must take the risk to open up and tell their feelings to others; then the group must respond (second step) in a positive way to what has been expressed. The second step is the most crucial. If a person risks and then is rebuffed by the group, he or she may not open up again until trust can be established once more. But if the group members respond positively, the individual develops confidence in them and will probably trust them with progressively deeper sharing in the future. Since opening up involves the trust factor, it's important for a student to feel safe, to test the waters, and to first share non-threatening material before moving on to some of his or her deeper feelings and thoughts.

Unfortunately, most students don't naturally open up. Over the course of their lives, students have been taught directly and indirectly to protect themselves—to be "on guard." In most youth groups, strategies and exercises are needed to help the group open up.

This chapter contains 22 exercises to help group members open up and get to know one another. These activities will contribute immensely to your process of building community. The exercises will help students feel comfortable with each other and feel more positive about the group.

How to Use the Opening Up Exercises

1. *Talk to the students about the need to listen.* Before you begin the opening up exercises, share some listening skills with them. For example: Listen as intently as possible to the person sharing; be an encouraging, responsive listener; look with loving eyes and a warm heart; listen in the same manner that you would like people to listen to you; be an active listener by nodding your head in agreement and understanding and by asking clarifying questions.

Some examples of clarifying questions are: "I don't quite understand, could you explain a little more about that?" "I'm interested, would you tell me a little more?" Discourage the listeners from thinking through their own answers or responses while another person is sharing. They need to be "all there" when someone else is speaking.

2. *Display acceptance rather than confrontation.* Don't use these exercises as "teachable moments" to capitalize on the moment to give a valuable lesson or make an important point. When a person shares from the heart, he or she needs to experience acceptance first despite his or her failures. If a student tells about his drinking problem, we, as leaders, don't need to preach a sermon on the evils of drink. We need to listen. Let the student come to you later for advice. But at this second stage in the process of building community, confrontation can be too threatening and can short-circuit your intended overall goals.

3. *Don't attempt to initiate a discussion about the information an individual shares.* Simply encourage the student to share. Ask clarifying questions if you don't understand what a person is saying. For most students, openness is related directly to how comfortable and secure they are feeling *at that moment.* Discussing what individuals have shared (unless the exercise specifically requests it) may be too threatening.

4. *Thank a person when he or she finishes sharing.* If a student is not given positive feedback, he or she may interpret silence as rejection.

5. *Model openness as the leader.* If we, as leaders, share on a

superficial level, group members will as well. Be the first person to share. Allow the youth to see some of your imperfections. The rest of the group will realize by your openness that it's acceptable not to be perfect; that God can *use* an imperfect person; and, better yet, that God can *love* an imperfect person. This suggestion, to go first and share your own thoughts, is directly opposite to the philosophy of bond building, in which you are cautioned not to express your opinions *during* the bond building exercises. (Of course, you can share during the discussion period that follows a bond building exercise.) In bond building, you want the group to work together without the "right answer" from you. In opening up, you want the students to see a model for openness—you!

6. *Facilitate the process of sharing.* If your group is not accustomed to sharing, you may want to ask a question and then go around the circle asking everyone to participate. A person can "pass" at any time and not share, but the circle strategy often makes the discussion environment less threatening because everyone expects to share. Equality exists; it might be scary, but it's fair.

7. *Use small groups.* The optimum group size for all of these exercises is five to eight people. A larger group will slow down the sharing and cause some participants to feel intimidated and overwhelmed. Large groups should split into smaller ones. (The estimated times for these activities are calculated for groups of seven people.)

8. *Be aware of the differing vulnerability levels.* Vulnerability can be defined as openness—the willingness to risk, to share even to the point of being misunderstood or hurt. To make these exercises effective, we, as leaders, need not move way beyond what the group can handle.

When initiating this step in building community, the first thing to do is to think about your group—as a whole and as individuals. Ask questions such as, "Where are we in the group building process?" "How well do our kids share with one another?" "Who in the group is reluctant to share?" "How can I help that person open up?"

Then look at the exercises and select ones that your group can handle at this stage. For instance, The Best (page 60) is very low on vulnerability. The questions, although good at helping students open up, are not demanding. On the other hand, Faith Collage (page 60) requires more openness and honesty to be effective.

Don't be *too* cautious or *too* hesitant. Young people are more open than we think. If you've spent some time on bond building and carefully followed the previous seven suggestions, these opening up exercises should be real winners.

With these thoughts in mind, let's open up.

THE BEST

Time: 45 minutes.
Materials: none.
Vulnerability: low.

Description

1. Have the group members form a circle.
2. Go around the circle and ask the first person the first question, the second person the second question, etc.
3. Go around the circle several times, rotating the questions.

Discussion

1. What was one of the best vacations you ever had? Why?
2. What was one of the best birthdays you ever had? Why?
3. What was the best Christmas you ever had? Why?
4. What was one of the best childhood experiences you ever had? Why?
5. What was one of the best presents you ever received? Why?
6. What was one of the best times you had in athletics or with a hobby? Why?
7. What was one of the best family times you ever had? Why?

FAITH COLLAGE

Time: one hour.
Materials: one pair of scissors and one paper sack for each student. You also will need several magazines and bottles of glue.
Vulnerability: medium.

Description

1. Distribute the materials to the group.
2. Have the participants take 15 minutes to each make a collage. From magazines, have them cut pictures and words that represent their current relationship with God; for example, bright sunshine, sparkling water and a few gray clouds. Have them glue these onto the outside of a paper sack.
3. Next, have the participants find symbols in the magazines of five things with which they are struggling in their faith. For example, a picture of a college could symbolize a question of what God wants a person to do with his or her future. Ask each youth to place these five symbols inside the sack. (Inform the students

that they will only have to share with the group one of the five symbols.)

Discussion

1. Explain your collage.
2. Pull out one of the five items from inside your sack and explain why you are experiencing difficulty in this area of your faith.

FAMILY TREE

Time: 45 minutes.
Materials: none.
Vulnerability: low.

Description

1. Gather the group in a circle.
2. Ask the participants to each describe *every* member of their family—highlighting their positive characteristics. Use the following questions:

Discussion

1. What hobbies do they have?
2. What sports do they enjoy?
3. What do you know of their long-range career goals?
4. How would you describe their current job?
5. What do they enjoy about school?
6. What do they not enjoy about school?
7. What is the most enjoyable time you have spent with them?
8. What are three characteristics you admire in them?
9. What activities do you like to do with them?

FANTASY ISLAND

Time: 15 minutes.
Materials: none.
Vulnerability: medium.

Description

1. Tell the youth that they will have the opportunity to create a fantasy identity.
2. Give the participants five minutes to prepare their fantasy identity according to the following questions:
  • Whom would you like to be?
  • Where would you live?

- How old would you like to be?
- What time in history (past, present or future) would you live?
- What would your personality be like?
- Who would you have as friends?
- What would be your occupation?

Discussion

1. Describe your imaginary person.
2. Tell the group why you chose those characteristics.
3. What is one thing you can do now to be more the person you wish?

FORCED CHOICE

Time: 30 minutes.
Materials: none.
Vulnerability: medium.

Description

1. Ask all of the group members to stand in the center of the room.

2. Tell them that they will describe themselves by deciding which of two opposite words *best* describes themselves.

3. Designate one side of the room for people to stand on who agree with the first option and the other side for those who agree with the second option. Do not allow people to remain neutral. They must stand to one side of the room.

4. After the first "forced choice," have the group members reunite in the middle of the room and give them two new options to choose from.

5. Continue this process. During some of these questions, ask one or two participants from each side to share their positions. If the group members split roughly in half on a question, have them get with a person of the opposite position and explain their choices.

6. Ask the youth, "Which of the following two words best describes you?"

lion/lamb	thinking/asking
pillow/rock	intense/mild
winter/summer	costly/free
day/night	work/play
journey/home	argue/agree
active/passive	flute/trumpet
competitive/cooperative	steak/hamburger

entertainer/challenger
adventurous/safe
social/spiritual

wisdom/luck
agony/ecstasy
group/individual

Discussion

1. Which choices were easy for you to make? Why?
2. Which choices were more difficult for you to make? Why?
3. What did you learn about yourself through this exercise?
4. How did you feel when you were one of only a few people on a particular side?

FORCED CHOICE—SCHOOL

Time: 30 minutes.
Materials: none.
Vulnerability: medium.

Description

1. Ask all of the group members to stand in the center of the room.
2. Tell them that they will decide which of two opposite words *best* describes their school experience.
3. Designate one side of the room for people to stand on who agree with the first option and the other side for those who agree with the second option. Do not allow students to remain neutral. They must stand to one side of the room.
4. After the first "forced choice," have the group members reunite in the middle of the room and give them two new options to choose between.

5. Continue this process. During some of these questions, ask one or two students from each side to share their positions. If the group members split roughly in half on a question, have them get with a person of the opposite position and explain their choices.

6. Remind students not to make a selection upon what their school is like but upon *their own individual feelings* about their school experience.

7. Ask the youth, "Which of the following two words best describes your personal experience with school?"

forget/remember	creative/traditional
rain/sunshine	self-oriented/others-oriented
tough/gentle	future/present
beginning/end	activities/knowledge
together/apart	sprinter/jogger
closed/open	leader/follower
hammer/nail	giver/taker
listener/talker	aggressive/passive
peace/anxiety	research/recreation
hearer/doer	old/new
helping/watching	world/local

Discussion

1. Which choices were easy for you to make? Why?
2. Which choices were more difficult for you to make? Why?
3. Were you able to ignore the sides other people were choosing or did they influence your decision?
4. What did you learn about yourself through this experience?
5. What insights did you learn by seeing other people's perceptions of their school experience?

THE GOOD, THE BAD AND THE UGLY

Time: 45 minutes.
Materials: paper and pencil for each person.
Vulnerability: medium.

Description

1. Distribute the paper and pencils.
2. Have the participants choose six events, either positive or negative, which have happened in the past five years that left a profound mark on their lives; for example, death of a loved one, receiving a drivers license, etc. Have them write these events on the paper.
3. For each event, ask the youth to write how that experience still affects their life today.

Discussion

    1. Ask the students to share with the group two of their answers. The other students can ask clarifying questions. Use the following questions to help facilitate the discussion:

    2. How was the experience positive or negative in the short term? long term? Why?

    3. To whom did the experience cause you to draw closer? Why?

    4. What did you learn about God? yourself? life? Why?

    5. What was the major benefit of this experience for you? Why?

    6. What was the major drawback of this experience? Why?

HIGHS—LOWS

Time: 25 minutes.
Materials: none.
Vulnerability: low.

Description

    1. Gather the group in a circle.

    2. Go around the circle and ask each member to answer the first question. Encourage other members of the group to ask questions to clarify or expand the individual's response.

    3. Repeat the process with the second question.

Discussion

    1. What was the highlight of this past week for you? Why?

    2. What was the low point of this past week for you? Why?

IF I SHOULD DIE

Time: 45 minutes.
Materials: none.
Vulnerability: medium.

Description

    1. Gather the participants in a circle.

    2. Go around the circle and ask each group member to answer the first question.

    3. Repeat this process throughout each of the five questions.

Discussion

    1. If you were to die tonight, what would have been:
- a highlight of your life?
- the person who influenced you the most?
- the best compliment you ever received?

• a low point in your life?
• one of the nicest things someone ever did for you?
2. Allow the others to ask questions to clarify or expand each individual's response.

INDIVIDUAL COLLAGES

Time: 45 minutes.
Materials: a pair of scissors and piece of construction paper for each person. You also will need several magazines and bottles of glue.
Vulnerability: low.

Description

1. Distribute the materials.
2. Ask each participant to take 20 minutes to make a collage out of magazine pictures and words describing who he or she is as an individual.

Discussion

1. Describe your collage and tell what the pictures and words represent.
2. What did you learn about yourself from this experience?

Variations

1. Ask the students to construct a collage that describes positive characteristics of their family.
2. Have the youth construct a collage that describes what they want to be in the future.
3. Instruct the group members to construct a collage with two different sides: one describing the aspects of themselves everybody knows; the other side describing aspects most people don't know.

MAGIC PAWNSHOP

Time: 35 minutes.
Materials: none.
Vulnerability: low.

Description

1. Gather the participants in a circle.
2. Ask each member of the group the following questions.

Discussion

1. If you had access to a magic pawnshop and could trade in two things about yourself for two traits you don't possess:
   • What two traits would you trade in?
   • What two traits would you get in exchange?
2. Have each person tell how he or she arrived at the answers.

MEMORY LANE

Time: 45 minutes.
Materials: none.
Vulnerability: low.

Description

1. Gather the youth in a circle.
2. Go around the circle and ask the group members to answer the first question. Allow the group to ask questions to clarify each individual's response.
3. Repeat the process throughout each of the five questions.

Discussion

1. What is one of your first memories?
2. What do you remember about the first house in which you lived?
3. What is an incident you remember from the fourth grade?
4. Who did you have a crush on, or who was your hero in grade school?
5. What is an incident you remember from seventh grade?

QUESTIONS

Time: 30 minutes.
Materials: hat, scissors and a photocopy of the list of discussion questions.
Vulnerability: medium.

Description

1. Use the scissors to separate the list of questions; place the questions in a hat.
2. Have each student pull out a question and answer it. Don't pass the hat on until the person is through sharing.
3. Continue going around the group until all of the questions have been answered.

Discussion

1. What is one of the most enjoyable times you have spent with your family this past year?
2. What is something you are looking forward to doing with your family within the next six months?
3. What are three qualities you greatly admire in your dad?
4. What are three qualities you greatly admire in your mom?
5. What is one tradition in your family?
6. What is something you really want out of life?
7. What is one of the best books (apart from the Bible) you have ever read?
8. What would a perfect day for you be like? What would you do?
9. If God were seated next to you, what three questions would you ask him?
10. What are three things that make you angry or frustrated?
11. When is one time when you have been aware of God's presence?
12. What is one thing which makes you happy?
13. What is one thing you fear?
14. What is one of your happiest memories? Explain.
15. What is a question you have about Christianity?
16. If Jesus were here on earth today, what would most distress him?
17. If you could ask Christ to change one problem in the world today, what would you like him to change?
18. Where's one of your favorite places to go with your friends?
19. What are two things you would do if you were president?
20. What are two secrets for a long-lasting friendship?
21. What was one of the most fun times you had with your friends this past year?
22. What is one food you can't stand?
23. How do you feel about living forever?
24. What are three qualities you want your friends to have?
25. What do you think life on earth will be like in 100 years?
26. How would you describe heaven?
27. What is one way parents could do a better job in bringing up their kids?
28. How much discipline do you think children really need? Why?
29. Do you agree that using punishment is the best way to gain cooperation from children? Why or why not?
30. What is one thing you could say about death?
31. What is your definition of sin?

32. What is one present you'd like to receive?

33. If you could travel anywhere in the world, where would you go? Why?

34. Why do you think people go to church?

35. What was a time this past month when you felt close to your dad or mom?

36. What are three activities you like to do with your brothers and sisters?

37. What are three things that make your family laugh together?

38. What is one favorite memory of the time spent with your family as a child?

39. What is one time when you felt especially close to your brother or sister? Why?

40. My favorite animal is . . .

41. Satisfaction is . . .

42. I am concerned about . . .

43. I get discouraged when . . .

44. I feel afraid when I think about . . .

45. I feel bored with life when . . .

46. My friends and I really have fun when . . .

47. Three activities I like to do with my friends are . . .

48. A pet peeve of mine is . . .

49. When I have free time, I like to . . .

50. My favorite television program is . . . because . . .

51. My favorite food is . . .

52. In school, I like to . . .

53. Today I feel . . .

54. My ideal vacation would be . . .

55. My favorite song is . . .

56. The people I like best are . . .

57. In 10 years I see myself as . . .

58. Prayer is . . .

59. Forgiveness is . . .

RAINBOW OF FEELINGS

Time: 30 minutes.
Materials: a copy of the handout and a pencil for each person.
Vulnerability: medium.

Description

1. Pass out a pencil and a copy of the following handout to each group member:

> Choose four of the following emotions. Describe a situation in

> your life in which you experienced each of the four emotions.
>
> | | |
> |---|---|
> | angry | depressed |
> | like laughing | like crying |
> | afraid | bored |
> | extremely happy | overwhelmed |
> | crazy | nervous |
> | restless | useful |
> | loved | peaceful inside |
> | motivated to change | |

2. Allow 10 to 15 minutes to complete the handout.

Discussion

1. Share two of your answers.
2. Did you make any new discoveries with this exercise? Explain.

SIGNIFICANT OTHERS

Time: 30 minutes.
Materials: none.
Vulnerability: low.

Description

1. Ask the group members to think of four people who have had a significant influence on their life either in person or by learning or reading about them.
2. Ask each member the following questions:

Discussion

1. How did you get to know them?
2. What has impressed you about them?
3. How would your life have been different if you hadn't known them?

SYMBOLS

Time: 20 minutes.
Materials: none.
Vulnerability: low.

Description

1. Give the group members five minutes to each find an object that represents some aspect of his or her current relationship with God.

The young people may look for their ideas inside or outside.
2. Gather the class for discussion.

Discussion

1. Show the object you found.
2. How is it representative of your relationship to God?

Variation

Ask the youth to find an object that represents some aspect of their relationship with their mother, father or own self at this point in their life.

THREE MINUTES

Time: 45 minutes.
Materials: none.
Vulnerability: medium.

Description

1. Give each student three minutes to share with the group about himself or herself. The person can tell anything that he or she wishes. Encourage the person to tell things which few, if any, of the group members know.
2. If students have difficulty filling the three minutes, give them general topics to talk about such as family, hobbies, favorite sports, friends, thoughts about God, etc.
3. Do not cut anyone off when his or her three minutes are up. Some people will speak longer. This is to be encouraged.

Discussion

1. Was this exercise difficult to do? Why or why not?
2. What surprised you about this activity?

TRIAD BOOKLETS

Time: 15 minutes.
Materials: a booklet for each group of three (see below).
Vulnerability: medium.

Description

1. Prepare a number of booklets by photocopying the following pages, cutting them apart and stapling them together.
2. Divide the group into triads (groups of three). Give each triad a booklet.
3. Tell the youth that each person in the triad is to answer each question.

Discussion

1. Directions: Have each person answer the following questions—take turns going first.	2. To make life better, I would like to invent . . .
3. What I liked best about today is . . .	4. A time when I was very happy was . . .
5. I feel frustrated when . . .	6. When I think about the future I see myself . . .
7. One thing that I treasure most in life is . . .	8. Something I always have wondered about is . . .
9. To me, God is like . . .	10. I feel rebellious when . . .
11. I feel lonely when . . .	12. One thing that I enjoy about life is . . .
13. One thing that depresses me about life is . . .	14. If I could change one thing about myself I would . . .
15. Something I like about myself is . . .	16. One thing I regret having done is . . .
17. To keep from being hurt I . . .	18. Two things for which I am thankful are . . .

WHAT DO YOU THINK?

Time: 30 minutes.
Materials: a pencil and a copy of the discussion questions for each person.
Vulnerability: medium.

Description

1. Distribute the pencils and questions.

2. Give the participants 10 minutes to answer the questions.

3. When finished, read each question to the group, and have the individuals stand up according to the answer they selected.

4. Ask people to share why they answered as they did.

Discussion

Circle the answer which most closely resembles your opinion.

1. It would be most difficult for me to live with:
   - a. only being able to take a shower or bath once a week
   - b. no television
   - c. having to walk wherever I went

2. The constitutional right I would most be willing to give up is:
   - a. voting
   - b. freedom
   - c. other

3. When I have a disagreement with someone I usually:
   - a. want to discuss it with him or her
   - b. keep it inside
   - c. talk to a friend about it

4. What annoys me most is:
   - a. dirty dishes in the sink
   - b. wearing dirty clothes
   - c. listening to dirty jokes

5. My ideal summer would consist of:
   - a. working at a camp
   - b. going to Europe
   - c. making $10 an hour

6. My favorite meal is:
   - a. steak and potatoes
   - b. hamburger
   - c. exotic foreign food

7. What the world needs most is:
   - a. love
   - b. food
   - c. justice

8. I would like to live in the:
   - a. city
   - b. country
   - c. mission field

9. I would like to drive a:
   - a. truck
   - b. Porsche
   - c. Volkswagen Bug

10. When I start my own family I would like to:
    - a. adopt
    - b. have none
    - c. raise four of my own

11. After school I like to:
    - a. participate in a sport
    - b. have a job
    - c. have no commitments

12. My idea of a good book is:
    - a. comic book
    - b. science fiction
    - c. romance

13. I most like to watch on television:
    - a. educational TV
    - b. sports
    - c. news

14. For an ideal vacation I would like to:
   a. visit Hawaii   b. go skiing   c. visit an old friend or relatives

15. My favorite charity takes care of the:
   a. poor   b. sick   c. lonely

16. My idea of a good party is:
   a. my place—watch some videos and eat junk food   b. go to the lake—water-ski and eat hotdogs

17. I would like to be stereotyped as being:
   a. cool, calm and collected   b. warm, friendly and caring

18. I prefer to:
   a. have a lot of casual friends   b. have a few very close friends

19. I take life rather:
   a. seriously   b. casually

20. Is it worse to be:
   a. unjust   b. merciless

21. I tend to:
   a. initiate conversation   b. wait for others to talk to me

22. I base my life more on:
   a. feelings   b. facts

23. In my dealings with others I would prefer to be:
   a. firm   b. gentle

24. A man gets caught stealing food to feed his family. He should be:
   a. given a job   b. put in jail for a month

25. It is most important to spend money on:
   a. the U.S. Defense   b. solving the drug problem   c. feeding those starving in Africa

26. The most detrimental thing you can do to someone is:
   a. beat up him or her   b. spread terrible lies about him or her   c. steal all his or her belongings

WHAT I ENJOY

Time: 45 minutes.
Materials: a pencil and a copy of the handout for each person.
Vulnerability: low.

Description

    1. Distribute a pencil and a copy of the following handout to each person.

---

    1. List 20 things you enjoy doing.

    2. Star those which you would like to do more often.

    3. Place a $ by those that limit you from doing them more often because of their cost.

    4. Circle the five you most like doing. With whom, where and when do you do each of these? What are the benefits and drawbacks of each of these?

---

    2. Give the participants five minutes to complete the handout.

Discussion

    1. Share your answers to the fourth question.

    2. What most surprised you about your answers?

WHO'S YOUR NEIGHBOR?

Time: 40 minutes.

Materials: none.

Vulnerability: low.

Description

    1. Gather the participants in a circle.

    2. Ask a student one of the following questions about the person seated to his or her right. The person must answer the question as he or she thinks his or her neighbor would answer it. (The point of this exercise is not to have the student necessarily know the right answer, but to have fun guessing.)

    3. Once the student has responded, allow the neighbor to give the correct answer. (Encourage the person to go into detail explaining the correct answer.)

    4. Go around the circle in this manner twice, asking different questions of each individual.

Discussion

1. In what sport does he or she most enjoy participating?
2. What was the best vacation he or she ever had?
3. What is his or her favorite television show?
4. Given an afternoon totally unplanned, what would he or she do?
5. What musical instruments can he or she play?
6. Is he or she a "morning" person or an "evening" person?
7. What is his or her favorite summer activity?
8. What sort of items does he or she collect?
9. If he or she could visit any spot in the world, where would he or she go?
10. Who is his or her favorite teacher? Why?
11. What does he or she like about himself or herself?
12. Of what is he or she proud? Why?
13. If he or she had a million dollars, what would he or she do with it?
14. What is something that really bores him or her?
15. What gives him or her the most satisfaction?
16. If he or she could be anybody (past or present), who would he or she be?
17. What is something that he or she is looking forward to doing in the next six months?
18. What present would he or she like to receive?
19. What does his or her dad do for a living? mom?
20. Of what is he or she afraid?
21. If he or she could have any job, what would it be?
22. What television star would he or she like to be?
23. What really frustrates him or her?
24. To what place would he or she like to move?
25. What talent does he or she wish he or she had?

YEAR IN REVIEW

Time: 30 minutes.
Materials: none.
Vulnerability: medium.

Description

1. Gather the students in a circle.
2. Go around the circle and have the group members answer the first question. Allow the group to ask questions to clarify or expand the individual's response.
3. Repeat this process throughout each of the seven questions.

Discussion

1. What are two of your accomplishments this past year?

2. What was the highlight of this past year for you with your family?

3. What was the highlight of this past year for you with your friends?

4. What was a disappointment you experienced during this past year?

5. Who is the person who has influenced you the most during this year?

6. What was a lonely moment you had this past year?

7. What is one apprehension you have about the upcoming year?

CHAPTER 4:
AFFIRMING

Scene One

Sara's face beamed with joy as she heard the compliments directed toward her. "You have such a sweet, tender spirit. You really care about people." Sara was no ordinary 14-year-old. She lived on the streets making her living as a prostitute—life was anything but a joyful experience for her. This time of affirmation at the drop-in center for street kids was changing her life. She was beginning to see herself through God's eyes. Her eyes sparkled as she began to believe that a hope for her future existed.

Scene Two

Randy, a quiet, reserved junior, showed little of his inner feelings or true self to the group. It wasn't until he heard his peers telling him how much they appreciated him that he felt the freedom to be transparent with his feelings. It wasn't until the group members verbalized how they loved him that he was able to share his imperfections with them. Slowly he began to come out of his shell. As he received affirmation from the group, his growth as a person accelerated.

Mark Twain once said, "I can live for two months on one good compliment." But most of us rarely receive Twain's "good compliment." Indeed, we seldom compliment *ourselves*. Instead, we blast ourselves for the slightest mistake and ignore our positive qualities. We practice being negative so often that we see our cup as one-quarter empty instead of three-quarters full. Without positive reinforcement, we become confused and disenchanted with our lives.

People who seldom receive affirmations are frequently defensive, cynical, apathetic and bitter. Yet when someone sees and affirms positive characteristics in them, important needs are fulfilled: the need to be appreciated, the need to be honored, the need to be affirmed. When these needs are met, the individual is more free to be the person that God intended him or her to be.

The Apostle Paul recognized people's need for affirmation. In his Epistles, he constantly complimented others for their attitudes and good deeds. He instructed the followers of Jesus to do the same, "Therefore encourage one another and build one another up, just as you are doing" (1 Thessalonians 5:11).

In Claude Steiner's children's story **A Warm Fuzzy Tale**, the people of the local town discover the healing power of compliments ("warm fuzzies"). Dissension dissipates in this fairy-tale town when the people care enough to tell how much they appreciate each other.

Affirmations are also important to the health of the youth group and the individual members. The 18 affirming exercises in this chapter are designed to encourage group members to express their appreciation for one another and to encourage health and healing in the group. Students may find it difficult to give compliments because of the insecurities they feel in their own lives and because of the cultural climate in which they live. Rather than affirmations, criticism and put-downs may come more naturally to them. These 18 exercises have been designed to facilitate complimenting others. These exercises help youth group members to concentrate on the positive characteristics of their peers and to affirm one another.

How to Use the Affirming Exercises

1. *Set the stage for affirmations.* You will create the climate of love and acceptance even before the first exercise is done. Be affirming, loving, accepting. Be careful not to use put-downs. They're killers. Don't be afraid to tell members of the group, "I love you." Affirm them in as many ways as you can; be an example of affirmation.

Since the setting in this step is totally affirming, don't capitalize on teachable moments. Don't look for opportune moments to teach the youth valuable lessons. Merely compliment, affirm and accept them.

2. *Ask students to speak directly to the person they are affirming.* Ask the youth to use first-name vocabulary. For example, "Tom, you really are a good listener." Not, "He listens well." Although speaking directly to the person is difficult; it is necessary to make the affirmations ring true.

3. *Encourage the students to keep all of their comments positive.* The following comment could do more harm than good: "I'm surprised by how well you have fit in this group since you aren't as athletic and witty as the rest of us." Put-downs that are cloaked in affirmation are still put-downs.

4. *Encourage the students to accept the compliments given to them.* Remind participants of the rule in affirming exercises: Compliments cannot be denied; they are simply statements of how one person perceives the other. A person's perceptions are not debatable. A simple "thank you" is the best response to an affirmation. Anything more or less is unnecessary.

5. *Ask individuals to be specific in their compliments.* Instead of, "I like your attitude," encourage the students to say, "I like the way you are so conscious of people's needs and try to serve them." Ask the youth to give specific examples such as, "The other day I saw you helping a freshman who had dropped his books all over the hall." Examples help keep the receiver from denying the truth of the affirmation.

6. *Discourage students from complimenting uncontrollable characteristics.* Compliments should focus on internal characteristics or external actions. Giving positive feedback about physical appearance, for example, often causes a person's self-worth to rely on his or her attractiveness. Remember the following statement: "...man looks on the outward appearance, but the Lord looks upon the heart" (1 Samuel 16:7).

7. *Discourage individuals from using comparisons.* A person should not be told, "You're the smartest student in the tenth grade." This makes the person's success in life relative to the actions of others around him or her. A better affirmation would be, "I really appreciate your quick mind and the way you apply yourself in your studies. It's a real example to me. Thanks."

8. *As a leader, you also should participate.* Take the opportunity to affirm the youth and let the group members have the opportunity to affirm you.

9. *Write the affirmations.* Younger students have difficulty thinking of affirmations quickly. In advance, encourage them to write out their affirmations.

10. *Use various-size groups.* In all of these activities, any number of youth can participate:

11. *Include God.* An excellent method of teaching students how to praise God is to do these exercises and include God as one of the group members. For example, with the Affirmation Collage (page 81), ask the youth to make a collage describing the positive characteristics of God as well as members of the group.

Remember these suggestions as you and your group participate in the affirming exercises.

AFFIRMATION COLLAGE

Time: 45 minutes.

Materials: several markers, magazines, bottles of glue and scissors. You also will need one piece of construction paper for each person.

Description

1. Tell the students that they will be given the opportunity to make a collage describing the positive characteristics of each youth group member. They should not merely describe who the members are and what they do. They should key in on qualities such as enthusiasm, helpfulness, compassion, etc.

2. Give the students a few minutes to think of specific characteristics for each member.

3. Distribute the magazines, scissors and glue. Tell the youth to find words and pictures describing each member.

4. While the members are looking through the magazines, write each person's name on a separate piece of construction paper and place the papers at the front of the room.

5. Instruct each person to take the phrases or pictures describing each group member and glue them on the corresponding papers.

6. When finished, pass each collage around the room. Ask each participant to explain his or her contribution to each collage. Give the collage to the student it describes.

AWARDS

Time: 45 minutes.

Materials: ribbon, scissors, thin cardboard, glue, gold seals, crayons, markers, etc.

Description

1. Divide the class in half and appoint a leader for each group. Tell the students that they will be creating awards for each individual in the other group. The awards must focus on positive qualities and refrain from offensive humor and put-downs.

2. Distribute the materials.

3. Instruct each group to go to a separate room and brainstorm for ideas for an award for each individual in the other group. Have them use the art supplies to create the awards.

4. Reunite and hand out the awards one at a time. Explain how each award was selected.

CANDLE WITH CARE

Time: 20 minutes.
Materials: candle in holder and matches.

Description

1. Form a circle and light the candle.

2. Begin by holding the lighted candle and telling the group what you appreciate about one of the people in the circle. (Do not say who you are talking about.) When you are done, pass the candle to the person you described.

3. That person, in turn, shares about another person and passes the candle to him or her.

4. Continue this process until everyone has been affirmed twice.

5. As a leader, be careful to affirm individuals who otherwise may not receive affirmation from the group.

Variation

This exercise may be done without a candle. Have each individual share words of appreciation and then announce the name of the person. The announced person continues the process.

CELEBRATION

Time: 10 minutes.
Materials: 10 pieces of peppermint candy for each person.

Description

1. Give 10 pieces of candy to each person in the group.

2. Instruct the members to mingle with the group and give a piece of candy to different individuals, telling them what they specifically appreciate about them.

3. Tell the students to continue until all their candy is gone.

4. As a leader, plan ahead and make a point of affirming individuals who may get neglected.

Variation

This exercise is an excellent method of affirmation in a large group setting. The larger the group, the more candy you give to the members to distribute.

CHARACTER STRENGTH TREE

Time: 35 minutes.
Materials: a pencil and an enlarged "tree" handout for every member of the group. (The tree should be large enough for the students to write in it.)

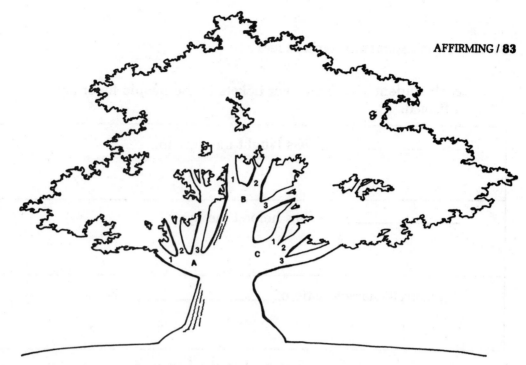

Description

    1. Divide the class in half and appoint a leader for each group.
    2. Give each person a pencil and a handout.
    3. Instruct the groups to go into separate rooms and collectively complete one "tree" for each member in the opposite group. Fill it out in the following manner:
a,b,c: three different positive characteristics of the individual
1,2,3: three specific incidents when the individual has displayed
        those character strengths
    4. Bring the two groups back together and show the Character Strength Trees to each individual, explaining in front of the group the details of each tree.
    5. Give each person the tree which describes him or her.

COMPLIMENTARY TICKETS

Time: 20 minutes.
Materials: one set of "tickets" and a pencil for each person. If you have more than 10 students, you will need more than one set of tickets for each person.

Description

    1. For each member, photocopy and cut out the set of "tickets" on the following page.
    2. Distribute the tickets and a pencil to each person.
    3. In the spaces provided, have the students write the name of *each* group member and finish the sentence about that person.
    4. Ask each person to share what he or she wrote. Then have

each student give his or her tickets to the people he or she affirmed.

_____ has taught me how to:
_____ has helped me by:
A positive characteristic of _____ is:
_____ is a good leader because:
What impresses me most about _____ is:
I am glad _____ is in our group because:
_____ has been influential in my life by:
_____ has helped me draw closer to God by:
I can tell _____ understands me because:
_____ has been a model to me in:

EULOGY

Time: 35 minutes.
Materials: a pencil and "eulogy" handout for each person.

Description

1. Divide the class in half and appoint a leader for each group.
2. Give each person a pencil and a copy of the following handout:

> Today we are gathered to pay tribute to _____,
>
> son/daughter of _____.
>
> _____ will be honored for . . .
>
> _____ has been admired by others for . . .
>
> _____ has always hoped he or she would . . .
>
> _____ will be missed by his or her friends because . . .

3. Instruct the groups to go into separate rooms and collectively write "eulogies" for each person in the opposite group.
4. Reunite the groups and read the eulogies out loud.
5. Give the eulogies to the individuals they commend.

FAMILY AFFIRMATION

Time: 30 minutes.
Materials: a paper and pencil for each person.

Description

1. Form a circle, then distribute a paper and pencil to each person.
2. Allow five minutes for each person to write seven qualities he or she admires about his or her parents.
3. Go around the circle and have each person share the qualities he or she admires.
4. After one person has shared, have the group pick out two of the qualities in that person's parents that the individual also portrays in his or her own life. Ask the group members to describe and affirm a time the individual demonstrated those qualities.

FUTURISTICS

Time: 35 minutes.
Materials: none.

Description

1. Give each person an opportunity to share what he or she sees in the future for each person in the group, and why.

2. Ask the following: "Given each individual's strengths, what do you imagine him or her doing 10 years from now? Be specific. What makes you think he or she will be doing that?"

3. Avoid negative responses. Make sure each individual receives equally encouraging answers.

GIFT CERTIFICATES

Time: 20 minutes.
Materials: "gift certificates" (see below) and pencils.

Description

1. Give the group members five to seven minutes to think of character strengths which they appreciate in each of the other members and would like to have for themselves. Emphasize that each person in the group has strengths that others don't have.

2. Give each person a pencil and as many "gift certificates" as there are people in the group.

3. Instruct the group members to go to an individual and state what character strength they would like from him or her. That person then writes out a gift certificate to them for that strength.

Gift Certificate

Being of sound mind and body, I, _____,

on this _____ day of _____, _____, hereby do give

to _____ some of my _____.

Signed _____

GIFTS

Time: 35 minutes.
Materials: none.

Description

1. Form a circle.

2. Give the group members five minutes to think how they will answer the following question:

If you could give each person in this group a gift (without thought of its actual feasibility), what gift would you give? For example, "Because of your adventurous spirit, I want to give you a set of eagles' wings so you can soar to new adventures." Or, "Because you love to travel, I want to give you an airplane ticket with unlimited mileage so you can travel any time." Or, "Because you love to pray, I want to give you a giant, shady oak tree to sit under and pray to God."

3. Go around the circle and have each person share what gift he or she wants to give each individual and why he or she chose that gift.

Variations

1. Use this exercise to give make-believe presents to an individual on his or her birthday.

2. Have everyone search the room and find a symbol of the fantasized gift. For example, a map could be a gift of free travel for a lifetime.

GROUP HUG

Time: two minutes.
Materials: none.

Description

1. This short exercise is a perfect method of closing a meeting in which the group has felt warmth and closeness toward one another.

2. Have the group members stand, form a line and place their arms around the people on either side of them.

3. Instruct the person at one end of the line to begin rolling, with his arms still around the people beside him, into the rest of the group—cinnamon-roll-style.

4. Once the group has wound up tightly, say, "One, two, three, hug!" The group all squeezes at the same time, giving one gigantic mass squeeze.

LEADER AFFIRMATION

Time: 45 minutes.
Materials: one 3x5 card for each member.

Description

1. Before a meeting, write individual notes of encouragement to give to each group member. Tell the students things you appreciate about them and ways you visualize achievement in their lives.

2. Distribute the notes as the students arrive to a meeting.

Variations

1. Obtain a "name" book from your local bookstore. On a 3x5 card for each student write what his or her name means, its spiritual connotation and a relevant scripture. Sign your name to the card. For example:

Cindy
"Moon"
Reflector of God's truth
Psalm 27:1 "The Lord is my light and salvation; whom shall I fear?"

Chris

2. Do another variation for volunteer leaders—mail it.

NAMES IN A HAT

Time: 15 minutes.
Materials: Write the name of each group member (including the leader) on separate slips of paper and place them in a hat.

Description

1. Ask each person to draw a name from the hat.
2. Have each student share something that he or she appreciates about that person.
3. Instruct each group member to keep his or her slip and pray for that person throughout the coming week.

NOMINATIONS

Time: 20 minutes.
Materials: a handout, pencil and Bible for each person.

Description

1. Distribute the Bibles, pencils and handouts (see below).

Eye: has the ability to perceive and understand what is happening around him or her.

Ear: listens in a caring manner. People come to him or her with their problems.

Mouth: is able to articulate and express well. Good speaking ability.

Head: coordinates others, administrates and organizes.

Foot: encourages action, gets a group moving toward completing the tasks at hand.

Hand: gives physical assistance and help. Serves others with joy.

Heart: has compassion and affection for others; is empathic.

Funny Bone: humorous, fun-loving and jovial.

Brain: contemplative thinker, finds the solution to problems.

Skin: holds the group together, peacemaker.

2. As a group, read aloud 1 Corinthians 12:12-27.

3. Have each individual fill out the handout, nominating each group member to one of the "body" parts.

4. Ask each person to read and explain his or her answers to the group.

TELEGRAMS

Time: 20 minutes.

Materials: paper and a pencil for each person.

Description

1. Give each person a pencil and enough pieces of paper for each group member.

2. Instruct the youth to write a "telegram" (a short note) to each person in the group telling what they appreciate about him or her. Encourage the writers to sign their names. However, if it is an extremely shy group, give the students the option to leave the notes unsigned.

3. Instruct the students to take off one of their shoes and place the shoes along the wall.

4. Use the shoes as "mailboxes" in which fellow group members may deliver their telegrams.

TEN

Time: 45 minutes.

Materials: paper and pencil for each participant.

Description

1. Form a circle. Distribute a paper and pencil to each person.

2. Allow five minutes for the students to write 10 things they like about themselves.

3. Have an individual read his or her list of 10 items. Allow three different individuals to share specific examples of how they have seen one of those 10 qualities in that person.

4. Go around the circle, giving each individual a chance to be on the "affirmation seat."

WARM FUZZIES

Time: 35 minutes.
Materials: none.

Description

1. Form a circle and ask one person to go to the center.
2. Go around the circle and have each participant share something he or she appreciates about the person in the "hot seat."
3. Continue until everyone has been affirmed.
4. Close this exercise with a prayer. Ask each individual to express what he or she appreciates about God.

Variations

1. For younger students who have difficulty sharing positive qualities about one another, it is helpful to have only the leaders do the affirming, while the rest of the group listens.
2. Have participants express what they have appreciated about the others in the group during a specific time period such as a weekend retreat, trip, special event, etc.
3. On someone's birthday (or when an individual is obviously having a rough day), have the group give warm fuzzies to that person only.

CHAPTER 5:
STRETCHING

Scene One

Fear engulfed Ron as he edged ever so slowly to the precipice of the 100-foot cliff and looked down. His rock climbing guides were asking him to use a safety system of ropes and rappel down the rock face. The guides assured Ron that the activity was safe, but Ron's fear was greater than their assurance. He began nervously sharing with the rest of the group his fear of heights. One of Ron's friends stepped to his side, put his arm around him and asked if he wanted to pray. Ron did.

After prayer, and with the support of his buddies, Ron apprehensively and hesitatingly clipped into the rope system and began his rappel. By the time he reached the bottom, he was ecstatic. With encouragement from the group, trust in God and some newfound courage, Ron had accomplished the seemingly impossible.

The experience had a profound impact on Ron's life because he had acknowledged a weakness and had overcome it with help from the group. The youth group took on a new meaning for Ron that day. Instead of being merely a gathering place for fun and games, it had become a group of people with whom he could share his struggles and receive their care. Ron felt a sense of deep satisfaction. He suddenly could relate the scripture ''bear one another's burdens'' to himself as well as to his own youth group.

Scene Two

''Safety First'' was the motto by which Susan and her family lived. Her dad had installed fire extinguishers at seven different locations around the house, had devised an escape plan in case of an emergency and had religiously required the family to wear seat belts in the car at all times. The family motto also was applied to their relationships with people. Her parents, her home, and her suburban high school had protected Susan from the dirt and grime of the city. She had been safe, but now her youth group was leaving for a night at an inner-city mission. Susan was extremely reluctant to go. Although she had argued with her parents and had finally convinced them of the safety of the group experience, she realized she had argued more to assert her own independence than because she wanted to participate in an inner-city service project. Deep down inside, she too believed in "Safety First," and she was apprehensive about going. What kind of people would she meet? What would they smell like? Would she be in danger? What if she wanted to run home early?

But Susan went to the mission; and her life was never the same. The culture shock *was* overwhelming; some of the people *did* smell. But Susan realized she wanted to help and she did. After the group returned to the church the next day, Susan made a commitment to make a difference. She and the youth group began monthly visits to the mission providing meals and a listening ear to the men and women. "Safety First" was replaced by "Service First" because Susan and her group had been stretched.

Most individuals need to be stretched. They need to be placed in unfamiliar situations where they can experience the authentic trustworthiness of God and their peers, come to grip with new realities and new strengths, face their weaknesses (with the support of their friends), become "overcomers," and face a situation that they formerly would have avoided. Not only *face* difficult situations, but *succeed.*

Stretching experiences fulfill these needs. They place the group members in situations where they must face and conquer obstacles. Group building occurs as people move out of their "comfort zones." In this new environment, their fear of the unknown causes them to turn to one another for support.

Stretching experiences can and do occur naturally among groups. For example, families experience extremely stressful periods in their development: financial difficulties, birth, death, marriage, divorce, sickness, value conflicts. Amazingly, many families bond together and grow stronger as a direct result of these circumstances.

Unfortunately, most youth groups don't exist as units for sufficient periods of time for these stretching experiences to emerge naturally. It then becomes imperative for us, as youth leaders, to create fun and challenging exercises that cause our group members to stretch, grow and learn. That's the purpose of this chapter. These 18 stretching exercises are provided for your use. The exercises come in different forms: some are service projects; some are adventure activities; and some fit into the category of "miscellaneous." The stretching experiences vary greatly in the amount of time they require and the locations in which they occur.

The exercises in this chapter are the most difficult in the book to prepare and execute. They are also some of the more worthwhile activities. They help to create an active learning environment that compels students to become involved in the exercises. These experiences will be etched vividly in the memories of participants for years and will help them mature in their walk with Christ.

How to Use the Stretching Exercises

1. *Schedule at least 30 minutes for discussion.* These activities invariably produce teachable moments—those opportune moments on which leaders can capitalize to make important points. After participating in stretching experiences, students are much more open to new challenges and to growth. They also are open to sharing because they have been through the first few steps in group building and they have gone through an intense experience together.

The discussion questions highlight the possible teachable moments per activity. Use the given discussion questions, alter them and add your own.

2. *Be aware of group size for maximum learning.* The optimum size for these events varies. Some of these exercises can involve only three or four individuals at a time without disrupting the purpose of the experience.

3. *Carefully choose the experiences.* Choose the stretching experiences that best will help your group. What proves to be stretching for one group may not be challenging for another. Use the knowledge you have of your group to make the choices.

4. *Call the contact person mentioned in these exercises.* These people are more than willing to help you plan and implement the exercise. Call and request their assistance.

5. *Be careful in your use of secrecy.* Use your discretion in deciding how much of an exercise will be kept secret from the participants and their parents. Some of the exercises will work best as total surprises; but secrecy with other exercises may cause some real problems. If in doubt, give advance warning.

6. *Follow the order of the discussion questions.* The questions follow a natural progression from first to last; they are numbered for maximum impact.

7. *Adapt or alter the experiences.* Depending on your location, some of these activities are more feasible to do than others. For example, due to cost and time, a group living in Nebraska may

opt to river raft rather than climb a mountain. Or that same group may decide to incorporate a stretching activity into their annual youth group trip. The group would simply plan meals, lodging, transportation and costs for the time it would take to travel to and from the site. Feel free to alter and adapt these exercises to fit your needs.

With these thoughts in mind, let's stretch!

ADULT NIGHT

Time: 90 minutes (preparation); two and one-half hours (activity).
Group Size: one student for every four adults.

Description

The students will lead an evening of group building exercises for the adults in the church. The adults will benefit from the opportunity to share and the teenagers will be stretched by leading people who are two and three times their age.

Preparation

1. Use the following program outline:

Time	Activity
15 Minutes	One Bond Building Exercise (Chapter 2)
35 Minutes	One Opening Up Exercise (Chapter 3)
15 Minutes	One Bond Building Exercise (Chapter 2)
35 Minutes	One Affirmation Exercise (Chapter 4)
15 Minutes	Trust Fall (page 53)
3 Minutes	Prayer
2 Minutes	Group Hug (page 87)
30 Minutes	Refreshments

2. Find a location for each group of adults where they will be able to be out of sight and sound from the other groups.

3. Gather refreshments for the last 30 minutes of the activity.

4. Gather materials needed for each exercise.

Before the Activity

1. During the week prior to the Adult Night, assemble the students for a 90-minute planning session. (If the students previously have not participated in the planned activities, lengthen the planning session and play the games. The students must be familiar with the exercises in order to lead them.) Do the following at the planning session:

• Discuss each exercise and how to lead it (include pitfalls to avoid).

• Decide which students will team up to lead a group. Have

them decide who will lead which games at the Adult Night.
 • Discuss the students' apprehensions about leading adults.
 2. Conclude the meeting with prayer for the upcoming Adult Night.

During the Activity

1. Place one student with every four adults. An ideal-size group is two students for every eight adults. Do not have students participate in the same group as their parents.
 2. It is important that the students lead the whole evening's activities. Youth sponsors should refrain from helping the students give instructions to the adults.
 3. Save 30 minutes at the end of the evening for the student leaders to discuss the activity while the adults are having refreshments.

Discussion

1. What happened tonight as you were leading your group?
 2. At what point did you feel the most uncomfortable being a leader?
 3. How did your co-leaders support you?
 4. What did you learn from this experience that you can apply to your everyday life?

COMMUNITY SERVICE

Time: one hour (preparation); four to eight hours (activity).
Group Size: any number.

Description

The students will spend a day traveling door-to-door in groups of four asking people if there is a job they can do as a service from the church such as yard work, baby-sitting, cleaning, etc. Not only will people in the neighborhood be ministered to by the servant attitude, but the participants themselves will be stretched. (Many youth find it difficult to approach and talk with total strangers.)

Preparation

1. Carefully select a community to visit. People in some areas are apprehensive about having unknown teenage visitors. Make your visit during a season in which there are plenty of outdoor jobs available. Some people may be apprehensive about strangers in their homes.
 2. Gather any necessary equipment such as lawn mowers, rakes,

garbage bags, buckets, sponges, soap, etc. Place all of this material at a designated location where the students can call and have it delivered to the place where they are working.

3. Assign several drivers to the task of delivering equipment.

4. Arrange transportation to the neighborhood.

Before the Activity

1. Give specific instructions to the participants regarding their behavior:

• They should tell each household who they are and what church they are representing.

• There is no limit regarding the number of houses they may visit. They should stay at one house until all of the work they've been asked to do is completed before traveling to the next home.

• Each group of four should stay together and not split up to work at different houses.

• The students should accept no money or gifts.

2. Ask each participant to share how he or she feels about the upcoming time of serving door-to-door with the group.

During the Activity

1. Begin with a prayer for the people the students will make contact with during the day.

2. Divide into groups of four. Proceed to the neighborhood and begin the work day.

3. Meet at a designated place and time after the day for one hour of discussion.

Discussion

1. What specific service projects did you do?

2. Which person in your group was the main spokesperson?

3. What were people's initial reactions to your offer of service?

4. Was this stretching exercise difficult for you to do? Explain.

5. At what moment were you most apprehensive today?

6. How would today have been different if you had to go to these houses by yourself?

7. What did this experience teach you about serving others?

8. How can you apply what you learned today to your everyday life?

CROSS-COUNTRY SKIING

Time: one hour (preparation); overnight (activity).
Group Size: five to 10.

Description

The participants will wear backpacks, ski along snow-covered trails and endure cold temperatures. Participants will be challenged to overcome their frustrations of falling and trying to get up with a heavy pack. Compassion for one another will be encouraged as group members will help one another through the course of this activity.

Preparation

1. Contact a reputable cross-country ski guide service in your area. Contracting with a guide service is especially important in areas of high avalanche danger.

2. With your guide, share the goals of your outing and how you hope to accomplish them. Discuss the goal of helping the participants develop compassion toward one another.

3. Remind the participants to dress warmly for this outing. Dress in layers—wool bunting and polypropylene are preferable to cotton. Wool hats, socks and gloves are essential.

4. Require each minor to have a release form signed by his or her parent or guardian.

5. Prepare one of two options: Rent a lodge that requires students to ski at least a mile to reach, or take tents and sleep outdoors. In tents the stress element is high but also greatly productive. If you choose to spend the night outdoors, it is essential that you have an experienced wilderness guide with you.

6. Choose two or three bond building games to begin the day. Find games that stress compassion such as Radioactive Swamp (Chapter 2).

7. Bring enough food and water for the group. Ask the students to bring adequate sleeping bags and extra clothing.

8. Arrange transportation to and from the area.

Before the Activity

1. Have each participant share with the group his or her feelings about skiing and being out in the snow. Divide into groups and ask the students to pray specifically for the needs of the person on their left.

2. Tell the group members that they should travel together— only skiing as fast as the slowest skier. (This is an *important* program element to build group cohesiveness.)

3. Emphasize that cross-country skiing should be fun, challenging and invigorating. It creates the opportunity to learn about perseverance and compassion for others, one's own limitations and a broader perspective of the nature of God.

During the Activity

1. Play two or three bond building games, then leave for the ski area.

2. Allow at least an hour at the end of the event for discussion.

Discussion

1. Did you enjoy your time skiing? Explain.

2. What frustrations did you encounter?

3. How did you react when someone else got cold or tired and complained more quickly than you did? Would your feelings have changed if this factor threatened to spoil your day?

4. How did you react to being in a position to show compassion to others?

5. Was someone always there to help you up after you had fallen? How did it feel when people skied past you? What did it feel like when they helped you up? How does this relate to your personal life? How does it relate to your relationship with God?

DIVORCE

Time: 30 minutes (preparation); two hours (activity).
Group Size: three to 20.

Description

The students will go to the courthouse to observe divorce proceedings. This activity will be used as a stimulus for a discussion about divorce. The exercise will prove most effective as it opens the door for the group to rally around those students who have experienced a divorce in their family.

Preparation

1. Call the county courthouse and ask the county clerk what time during the week they hear divorce trials. Most courts hold all of the divorces during the same hour each week.

2. The majority of these "dissolutions" are "uncontested"—all the decision making regarding property and child custody has been done by lawyers out of court. The appearance before the judge is merely routine. It is not uncommon to witness as many as six uncontested divorces in a 45-minute period. The seeming ease with which certain people divorce is eye-opening.

"Contested" divorces are longer and more emotional. These are ones which are brought before the judge with portions of the settlement still unresolved. If you explain your purpose to the county clerk, he or she may be willing to "tip you off" to a divorce on the calendar which is contested. A judge may reserve the right to clear the courtroom of students if an argument becomes too heated. Both contested and uncontested divorces are educational and worth viewing by your students.

3. Provide transportation to and from the courthouse.

Before the Activity

1. Explain to the students that you are taking them to divorce trials to help them develop a greater awareness of divorce in our society.

2. Discuss the issue of divorce and how the students feel about it.

During the Activity

1. Proceed to the courthouse.

2. At the end of the event, allow 30 minutes for discussion.

Discussion

1. How did observing the divorce process make you feel?

2. What personal experiences were you reminded of through this activity?

3. What effect does divorce have on the children involved? What effect has it had on those of you who have experienced a divorce in your family?

4. How can being involved in a youth group help you through the pain of a divorce in your family?

5. How can divorce be prevented?

6. What can you be doing now to give your future marriage a better chance of survival?

7. What kind of a mark will this experience leave on you?

Note: Questions 5 and 6 are best used for older high school students.

HARD BARGAIN

Time: one hour (preparation); four hours (activity).
Group Size: 10 or more.

Description

The students will attend a meeting in which they must use play money to pay for various activities. Play money will be randomly distributed to participants through playing a game of UNO at the outset of the exercise. This event will challenge the students to treat others with compassion and to think of the needs of others before themselves.

Preparation

1. Gather one UNO game for every five students.
2. Make play money for the participants, or use Monopoly money.
3. Arrange for transportation to and from a swimming pool.
4. Buy ingredients to make pizza (or buy frozen pizza). You also will need utensils, napkins, plates, cups, pop, etc.
5. Gather a projector, screen and short 20-minute film.
6. Choose an affirmation exercise to play at the end of the activity (Chapter 4).

Before the Activity

1. Do *not* tell your students about the details of the evening's program. Simply inform them that it will be fun, extremely unusual and challenging.
2. Have an in-depth preparatory staff meeting. To make the event successful, it is essential that all staff members participate enthusiastically in *all* aspects of the evening along with the students. Following is a schedule of the evening's activities:

4:00 p.m.	Arrive and play UNO.
4:30 p.m.	Hand out money. Leave for swimming ($50 for ride to pool).
4:45 p.m.	Swim ($200).
6:00 p.m.	Arrive back at church ($50 for ride from pool). Pizza dinner ($100 per slice for first two slices, $150 per slice thereafter; $50 for utensils, plates, etc. Drinks are "on the house").
6:30 p.m.	Short movie ($100).
6:50 p.m.	Distribute free food.
7:00 p.m.	Debrief (see the discussion questions).
7:30 p.m.	Affirmation exercise (Chapter 4).

During the Activity

1. As soon as the students arrive, instruct them to get into groups of five and play UNO.
2. Stop the game after 20 minutes. Have the members in each group add up their scores and determine first through fifth places. Give play money to the students as follows:

first place = $1200

second place = $900
third place = $600
fourth place = $300
fifth place = $0

3. Tell the students that everyone will be required to use their play money to purchase the evening's activities. If the participants don't have enough "cash," they may obtain money from others by begging, bartering or working for them. (This statement must be carefully worded to give them the idea of how to obtain money without endorsing any particular method for its transferal.)

4. Tell the students only about the beginning of the schedule: $50 to ride to the swimming pool; $200 to swim; $50 to ride home from the swimming pool.

5. At dinner time, inform the students that they may work for "welfare checks" ($100 to prepare dinner and $100 to wash dishes).

6. Competition and stealing may develop. Allow this unless it gets violent.

7. Keep an eye out for any students who may seem hurt emotionally by this type of program. Seek them out and encourage them as needed.

8. Show a brief 20-minute movie. Do not tell the students that this is the last paid event.

9. Before debriefing the activity, distribute pizza and other food free of charge. (Don't let them know you are going to do this beforehand.) It is important for the students to have full stomachs before discussing the negative aspects of the event.

10. Carefully debrief this activity. Some students may feel "set up," and will justify their selfish behavior. Both those with and without much money will have exhibited selfish attitudes through hoarding, stealing, pouting, etc. This activity often creates hostile feelings between group members. Be sure to spend the time to care for the hurt feelings.

11. Conclude with an affirmation exercise (Chapter 4).

Discussion

1. Which side of the financial scene were you on? Were you a "have" or "have not"?

2. What did it feel like to have the financial status and situation you did?

3. What selfish attitudes did you personally show or feel during this event?

4. Which of these best describes your behavior this evening:
• I looked out for my own personal interests.

• I looked out for the interests of others.

5. How did your behavior affect the mood of the group?

6. How did your actions typify your everyday behavior?

7. In general, what are the costs and what are the benefits of looking out for your own personal interests?

8. In general, what are the costs and what are the benefits of looking out for the interests of others?

9. Read 1 John 3:16-18 and discuss its significance to your role in this event. How does this scripture apply to you?

10. Read Colossians 3:22-24 and talk about its relationship to your role in this event. How does this scripture apply to you?

11. How do you want your behavior to change as a result of what you've learned about yourself this evening?

HARD BARGAIN—A RETREAT VARIATION

Time: three hours (preparation); one weekend (activity).
Group Size: 15 or more.

Description

Students will attend a retreat in which they must use play money to purchase all of the goods they will need for the camp. Play money will be randomly distributed to participants through playing a game of Monopoly at the outset of the retreat. This event will challenge students to treat others with compassion, to think of the needs of others before themselves, and to reflect on the rich and the poor in modern society.

Preparation

1. Gather one Monopoly game for every five students. You also will need extra play money.

2. Schedule a time for your group to go to a church camp or retreat center.

3. Tell the students to gather additional supplies such as sleeping bags, towels, wash cloths, etc.

4. Arrange for a special speaker. Read the retreat to know what additional supplies are necessary.

Before the Activity

1. Do *not* tell your students about the retreat's program. Simply inform them that the weekend will be fun, extremely unusual and challenging.

2. Have an in-depth staff preparatory meeting. To make the retreat successful, it is essential that all counselors and staff (including the director) participate enthusiastically in *all* aspects

of the weekend along with the students. Following is a sample schedule:

Friday

7:00 p.m.	Campers arrive, play Monopoly.
8:00 p.m.	Instructions for the weekend's economic system.
8:30 p.m.	Organized recreation.
9:30 p.m.	Free time ($100 snacks available). Welfare station open (bricks and wheelbarrows).
10:00 p.m.	General session with speaker.
11:15 p.m.	Cabin time.
11:45 p.m.	Lights out.

Saturday

6:00 a.m.	Welfare station open (until breakfast).
7:00 a.m.	Counselor meeting.
7:30 a.m.	Rise and shine.
8:00 a.m.	Breakfast and KP.
8:30 a.m.	Cabin time/quiet time.
9:15 a.m.	Seminars.
10:15 a.m.	General session with speaker.
11:15 a.m.	Welfare station open.
Noon	Lunch and KP.
12:30 p.m.	Welfare station open.
1:00 p.m.	Organized recreation.
2:00 p.m.	Special party ($500 tickets). Includes cake, cookies, special entertainment such as a video movie (servers at the party get paid $150).
4:00 p.m.	Party ends.
5:30 p.m.	Announce the completion of the exercise (do not let this information out ahead of time). Give the participants a free dinner (nicely prepared, candlelight, counselors do KP).
7:00 p.m.	Meet in small groups and answer discussion questions.
8:00 p.m.	Everyone gathered together for students to share what they learned from the experience.
8:30 p.m.	Free time.
9:00 p.m.	General session with speaker.
10:15 p.m.	Cabin time.
11:00 p.m.	Lights out.

Sunday

7:00 a.m.	Counselors meeting.
7:30 a.m.	Rise and shine.
8:00 a.m.	Cabin time.
9:00 a.m.	Brunch.
10:00 a.m.	Affirmation exercise (Chapter 4).

11:00 a.m.   General session with speaker.

Noon   Pack up and go home.

During the Activity

1. As soon as the students arrive at the camp, tell them to drop their bags and go into a room full of Monopoly games. Without letting them know the purpose, instruct them to play Monopoly.

2. The director of the retreat and two or three helpers should spend 10 minutes locking up all of the luggage and sleeping bags before joining the others to play Monopoly.

3. Stop the game after an hour. Have the students trade in all of their hotels and property for cash. Instruct them to gather in another room, cash in hand.

4. Tell the students that everyone will be required to use their Monopoly money to survive and enjoy the retreat. If they don't have enough "cash," they may obtain money from others by begging, bartering or working for them. Those *with* money may do with it as they wish. (Note: This statement must be carefully worded to give them an idea of how to obtain money without endorsing any particular method for its transferal.)

5. Inform the participants that they may go on "welfare" and earn $50 by pushing a wheelbarrow full of bricks approximately one-fourth mile.

6. Tell the students that to get their sleeping bags, they will have to pay $300; luggage costs $300 as well. (Give them their toothbrush, however.) Other aspects of the retreat will also cost: $300 for each meal; $50 for dessert; $100 for special snacks; $500 for a mid-afternoon party; $100 to play free time activities such as football.

7. "KP" duties should be assigned to the different cabins (doing dishes, sweeping floors, setting up chairs, etc.). These duties will tempt the rich to hire others to do their work (don't suggest this to them, however).

8. If students cannot afford a meal, they may eat bread and milk which you provide at a special table for the "poor." Do not allow giving away of food at meals. Only allow the giving away of money.

9. Competition and stealing may develop. Allow this unless it gets violent.

10. Keep an eye out for shy students who may become hurt emotionally by this type of program. Seek them out and encourage them as needed.

11. Besides the economic system, the retreat should be programmed quite similarly to a typical retreat (with a speaker, cabin

meetings, seminars, singing, recreation, skits, etc.).

12. Complete the "economic system" portion of the retreat before the second night's dinner. Serve the students a special dinner. Then have them gather together in small groups for a time of debriefing the experience. Have a leader in each group go through the discussion questions with them.

13. After discussing the activity in their small groups, bring the camp together and allow students to share with the entire group the things they learned from the experience.

14. The following day conclude the retreat with an affirmation exercise from Chapter 4.

Discussion

1. Which side of the financial scene were you on?

2. What did it feel like to have the financial status you did?

3. How did you handle your negative feelings that came up during this activity?

4. Which sentence best describes your behavior this weekend? How?

- I looked out for my own personal interests.
- I looked out for the interests of others.

5. How did your behavior affect the mood of the group?

6. How do your actions this weekend in any way typify your everyday life?

7. In general, what are the costs and what are the benefits of looking out for your own personal interests?

8. In general, what are the costs and what are the benefits of looking out for the interests of others?

9. Read 1 John 3:16-18 and discuss its significance to your role in this event. How does this scripture apply to your life?

10. How do you think this game accurately reflected what goes on in our society?

11. How did it feel to be on welfare?

12. How have your attitudes changed, if at all, regarding the rich and the poor?

13. Read Colossians 3:22-24 and talk about its relationship to your role in this retreat. How does this scripture apply to your life?

14. How do you want your behavior to change as a result of what you've learned about yourself this weekend?

MOUNTAINEERING

Time: two hours (preparation); one weekend—depending on the distance to and from the site (activity).

Group Size: six to 15.

Description

Students will climb a mountain. They will be roped together for safety. As a group, they will combat their physical limitations and encourage one another to reach the summit.

Preparation

1. Contact a reputable mountaineering guide service and ask them to lead your group. The mountain chosen should have an elevation gain of 3,000 to 4,000 feet from trail head to summit and should be either a Grade I glacier climb or a fourth-class rock scramble. (Most guide services will require participants to be at least high school age to undertake this venture.) The guide service must have stringent safety standards and a strict certification policy for its guides.

2. Inform the guide service of your goals—to have the group work together and climb as a unit to the summit. Make sure your guides realize your desire to keep this event from becoming a glorification of the "athlete." Mountaineering is unique in that being roped together requires the super athletes to slow down for the out-of-shape climbers. Therefore, all participants learn something: perseverance or patience.

3. For a summit party, gather goodies such as juice and trail mix. Plan to sing a worship song such as "How Great Thou Art."

4. Choose bond building, opening up and affirming exercises (Chapters 2 through 4).

5. Gather camping equipment and food. The amount of supplies depends on the distance to and from the site as well as the length of time you will be on the trip. Check with the guide service for suggestions on supplies and equipment. They will have a list of equipment that they will supply.

6. Arrange for transportation.

Before the Activity

1. Inform the group members of the equipment they will need and what to wear.

2. Have a meeting for all youth sponsors and parents. Inform them of the trip details.

3. Have all the participants (age 18 and under) complete a parental release form.

During the Activity

1. During the early portion of the climb, play bond building,

opening up and affirming exercises as time allows.

2. Have a "surprise party" on the summit. Bring out the goodies which you have carried in your pack. Before leaving the top, sing a worship song such as "How Great Thou Art."

3. Allow one hour or more for discussion.

Discussion

1. Which of these feelings did you have as you climbed the mountain? Explain each feeling—when and where you felt it most.

_____ fearful	_____ impatient
_____ ecstatic	_____ compassionate
_____ like giving up	_____ cared about
_____ not cared about	_____ "Why am I doing this?"
_____ close to others	_____ other

2. What were the benefits of being roped together? frustrations?

3. How does being roped together relate to the concept of the "body of Christ"? Discuss Romans 12.

4. Which of you accomplished more than you thought you could today? What struggles are you facing in everyday life that seem overwhelming?

5. How did this trip make you feel about those everyday problems?

6. How can faith help you overcome or cope with your problems?

NIGHT AT A MISSION

Time: one hour (preparation); overnight (activity).
Group Size: three to five (sometimes more, depending on the okay of the mission director).

Description

Students will spend an evening serving at a city mission for the homeless. The group also will sleep at the mission. Group members will gravitate toward one another when faced with the culture shock.

Preparation

1. Contact the director of an inner-city mission. Obtain permission for your group to spend an evening serving them and sleeping overnight. Although this request is somewhat unusual, the mission staff will generally be excited about your visit. Ask them about arrangements for eating and sleeping. They may request that you bring your own sleeping bags or food. Some missions have a

set fee for visiting groups.

2. Determine what space is available for female overnight guests. The majority of beds in missions are for males. Be sure you have adult sponsors of both sexes if you take a coed youth group.

3. Explain to the director your desire to allow your group the opportunity to serve and interact with people residing there.

4. Find out from the director exactly what ways your youth group can be of service. Most missions have chapel services which church groups may organize and lead. Youth groups also can help serve or prepare meals with the residents of the mission. The mission may need minor repairs your group could provide; for example, painting, roofing or weatherization.

5. Arrange for transportation to and from the mission.

Before the Activity

1. Tell the participants to wear casual clothes—they might get dirty working at the mission. Tell them not to bring extra luggage, only sleeping bags (if so directed by the mission staff).

2. Inform the parents of your plans.

3. When the participants arrive at the church ready to go to the mission, have them write out and then share what they expect for the following 20 hours regarding:
- what they will learn.
- what stereotypes they have of people at missions.
- what they are nervous about.

4. Remind students that they will be visiting real people. Ask them to key in upon what they think these people are feeling and experiencing.

5. Load the participants into vehicles to travel to the mission.

During the Activity

1. Once you arrive at the mission, have the participants meet with the mission director. Ask him or her to inform the youth where they will be sleeping and what they will be doing for the upcoming period of time. Inform the participants to take their orders from the mission director.

2. Allow 60 minutes after the activity for discussion.

Discussion

1. How was this experience different from the expectations you wrote down before the activity? similar?

2. In what ways did you find that you needed each other as a group to make this experience easier?

3. In what ways will this activity leave its mark on you?

PLANNING MARATHON

Time: (will vary according to the chosen activity).
Group Size: three to five per project.

Description

The students will do the behind-the-scenes organization and administration of an elaborate event. People working closely together on a project will find they need to communicate a great deal to achieve compromise in their decision making. Students' inner emotions will surface and discussion of these feelings will bring the group closer together.

Preparation

1. Decide on an activity to organize such as a banquet, party, retreat or outing.
2. Gather materials according to the chosen activity.

Before the Activity

1. Several weeks before the activity is to take place, go through the "five levels of planning an activity" with the students:
• Determine the needs of the group for which the activity is being planned.
• Set goals for the activity to meet the needs.
• Establish a program centered around the goals.
• List methods and materials needed to make the program possible.
• Organize and administrate, assigning tasks to individuals.
2. Allow the participants to plan the activity. Give them as much ownership (and freedom to fail) in the project as possible. With this particular exercise, it is more important that the participants have a chance to plan it than it is for the activity to be a raving success. Ask thought-provoking questions to partially steer them toward better solutions, but do not renege on your promise to allow them to be the decision makers.
3. Be observant about students' frustrations in the planning process. Allow them the freedom to make a few mistakes in their relationships with one another. This will help them realize their own misgivings about the way they deal with people. When these differences arise between participants, help them talk through the options and successfully reach joint conclusions.

During the Activity

1. Allow the students to follow through with their planning and preparation. Be there to assist, but let the youth lead.

2. Allow 45 minutes for discussion at the end of the activity.

Discussion

1. How did you feel about organizing this activity?

2. In what areas of the planning process were you the weakest? strongest?

3. How well could you have planned this activity alone? How did the group help you?

4. How do your skills in working with other people need to be improved? What skills were beneficial during this process?

5. How does your Christian faith impact the planning and doing of a big project?

PRISON VISIT

Time: 90 minutes (preparation); two hours (activity).
Group Size: six to 25.

Description

Group members will assist in a chapel service or participate in a recreational activity with inmates of a prison or juvenile detention center. Students tend to fear for their own safety as they are confronted by a lifestyle of which they are unaccustomed. This will cause them to bind together with their peers and to reach out to others. They also will gain a first-hand look at our penal system.

Preparation

1. Contact the chaplain of the institution you will be visiting. Obtain the following information:

• What is the procedure for getting into the institution?

• What can and cannot one bring into the prison?

• What are guidelines for the group's attire and conduct while there? For example, discussions to avoid, procedures for further contact between individuals, male-female friendship, etc.

• Do you need to send a list of your group's participants to the prison beforehand?

2. Arrange transportation to and from the prison.

Before the Activity

1. Discuss with the participants the purposes of visiting a prison: encouraging, serving, caring, sharing about Jesus, etc.

2. Give the group the guidelines received from the chaplain

regarding dress and conduct. Discuss the details of your visit.

3. Have each individual share with the group his or her apprehensions about the activity.

4. Pray for the activity, for the overcoming of fears and for the opportunity to minister to the people's needs.

During the Activity

1. Proceed to the prison and assist in the chapel service or participate in a recreational activity.

2. Allow 30 minutes for discussion after the activity.

Discussion

1. How did you feel during your time in the prison?

2. How would things have been different if you had come here alone?

3. How did being with this group help you overcome your apprehensions?

4. How has this experience helped you grow closer to this group?

5. What are the root problems in the lives of these inmates which have caused them to end up in this institution?

6. How do you feel about the prison system? What would you do to change it if you could?

7. Read Matthew 25:31-46. How does Jesus feel about prisoners?

8. What can you apply to your life from this experience?

PUBLIC SPEAKING

Time: one hour (preparation); 90 minutes (activity).
Group Size: three to six.

Description

Several students will give a talk in front of the church body or other large group. Their fear of speaking in front of people may be difficult for them to handle.

Preparation

1. Select three to six people to talk in front of a group. The size and type of group they speak to will vary according to their natural ability. Select a speaking assignment which will challenge yet not overwhelm them. Allow all of the speakers to talk at the same meeting. The exercise will lose its effectiveness for building

community if it is not a shared experience with other students.

2. Give the speakers a week or so to prepare a five-minute speech. Have them practice giving their talks to you beforehand.

3. Explain to the participants that the keys to being a good speaker are:

- being excited about your subject.
- believing it is important for the audience to hear what you have to say.
- knowing about your subject from personal experience.

Before the Activity

1. Have individuals who are going to be speaking get together immediately prior to their speeches and share briefly with one another how they are feeling about giving their speech.

2. Pray for one another.

During the Activity

1. Proceed with the speaking assignments.

2. Allow 30 minutes for discussion.

Discussion

1. How do you feel your speech went?

2. When you got in front of the audience, of what were you afraid?

3. How did receiving encouragement from others make this experience easier for you?

4. What do you want to remember most from this experience?

5. How does this experience help you with future witnessing of your faith?

ROCK CLIMBING

Time: 30 minutes (preparation); several hours—depending on the distance from the site (activity).
Group Size: any number.

Description

Students will climb up and rappel off of 75-foot to 100-foot rock cliffs safely protected by ropes and sit harnesses. Participants will be challenged to overcome their fear of heights or perceived physical limitations and turn to the other members of the group for support and encouragement.

Preparation

1. Contact a rock climbing guide service with a quality reputa-

tion. Instruction by novices is dangerous. It is imperative that the selected guide service has a strict certification policy for its guides and is covered with adequate insurance.

2. Discuss with the guides your goals for the activity. Share with them your desire not to see which in the group are most athletic, but to build group cohesiveness through encouragement, cheers and hugs as students overcome their own perceived limits. Students should not be forced to do anything against their will— merely gently encouraged to step out of their "comfort zones."

3. Instruct the students to wear baggy pants, tennis shoes and other items suggested by the guide service.

4. Each minor may be required to have a release form signed by his or her parent or guardian.

5. Emphasize to the group that rock climbing is fun and challenging, and creates the opportunity to learn about oneself, teamwork and one's relationship to God.

6. Arrange for transportation.

Before the Activity

1. Gather any necessary equipment.

2. Select two or three bond building exercises (Chapter 2).

3. Have each participant share with the group his or her thoughts about rock climbing and rappelling.

4. Divide into groups of four and have the youth pray for the person on their left.

During the Activity

1. Highlight the day of rock climbing by playing two or three bond building exercises to establish the idea of teamwork.

2. Allow 60 minutes for discussion at the end of the activity.

Discussion

1. At what moment did you feel most apprehensive today? frustrated?

2. Which of you accomplished more today than you thought you ever could? Explain.

3. How did you feel trusting your physical safety to someone?

4. What was it like to hold someone's physical safety in your hands?

5. How was it difficult for some of you to be placed in a position where you were forced to show your weaknesses or apprehensions in front of the group?

6. How did the encouragement given to you by others make climbing easier? (Be as specific as possible.)

7. What did you learn about trust and faith through this exercise?

8. How can you apply the things you've learned to your relationship with God?

ROPES COURSE

Time: 30 minutes (preparation); four to six hours (activity).
Group Size: six to 10.

Description

The students will participate in a series of events, tied into ropes which are suspended above the ground. These activities will be diverse enough to create a degree of difficulty for nearly all students. Some will have trouble with the exercises which require physical strength; while others will have difficulty with events stationed high off the ground. Students thus will have an opportunity to support and encourage others as they overcome their personal apprehensions. Participants will realize that they can do much more than they expected with the help of friends.

Preparation

1. Contact an organization which owns and operates a ropes course. Many camps either have a ropes course or know who does.

2. Discuss your goals with the ropes course guides. Share with them your desire not to see which in your group are most athletic, but to build group cohesiveness through encouragement. Participants should not be forced to do anything against their will, merely gently encouraged to step out of their "comfort zones."

3. Each minor may be required to have a parental release form signed.

4. Emphasize to your group members that the activity will be fun and a challenge—not a contest, but a group cohesiveness builder.

Before the Activity

1. When the students arrive at the ropes course and have an opportunity to look at it, gather them together and have them each share which portion of the course will be most difficult for them. Pray for one another.

2. Remind the students that encouragement through cheers, hugs and prayers will greatly help their fellow group members.

During the Activity

1. Proceed with the course.
2. Allow 30 minutes for discussion after the activity.

Discussion

1. Which part of the ropes course was most difficult for you? Describe your feelings as you went into it.
2. What thoughts went through your mind as you *completed* the ropes course?
3. How did the encouragement given to you by others make the ropes course easy for you?
4. How was it difficult to be in a situation where you showed weakness or apprehension in front of the group?
5. What did you learn about trust and faith through this experience?
6. How can you apply this concept to your relationships with people? God?

SHARING YOUR FAITH

Time: one hour (preparation); two hours (activity).
Group Size: any number.

Description

After a time of instruction and prayer, the group will go in pairs to share their Christian faith with strangers. This experience will allow people to hear more about God as well as stretch standards by forcing the youth to talk with strangers about their beliefs in a controversial subject. This will promote a fear of rejection in the youth which they will struggle to overcome.

Preparation

1. Contact your pastor and ask him or her to instruct the group members in the most beneficial method of sharing their faith.
2. For this activity, find a large public area such as a mall or beach.
3. Arrange for transportation.

Before the Activity

1. Discuss with the group members why it is important for them to share their faith. Use scriptures such as Matthew 28:18-20; Acts 1:8; Romans 10:13-17.
2. Instruct the group members how to share their faith. Ask the pastor to present ideas and have the youth participate in role playing.

3. Ask each person to tell the group about his or her fears about doing this activity.

4. Pray for the youth group members and the people they will meet. Ask God for wisdom and boldness in sharing.

During the Activity

1. Proceed to the public site. Have the students travel in pairs throughout the shopping area or beach. Instruct the pairs to alternate having one person approach an individual and share his or her faith, while the other person prays for the situation. Continue this process for one hour.

2. Allow 30 minutes for discussion.

Discussion

1. What happened during your hour of witnessing?

2. How did having a partner help you?

3. How did you help your partner?

4. Who do you need to be sharing your faith with in your everyday life?

5. Close with a prayer for those people to whom the group members shared and for continual boldness for the students.

THIRD WORLD DAY

Time: several hours (preparation); 24 to 30 hours (activity).
Group Size: any number.

Description

Both World Concern and World Vision have similar 24- to 30-hour programmed Third World Days that simulate for groups what it is like to live in poorer countries and go without food. Students will learn empathy for those who live in other parts of the world. These exercises will allow the students to experience some frustration and will allow them to deal with a few of their personal weaknesses.

Preparation

1. Contact one of the following organizations and ask for detailed information packets on how to plan a Third World Day for your youth group.

World Vision
Attn: "Let It Growl"
Box 0
Pasadena, CA 91109
1-800-423-4200

World Concern
Attn: "Refugee Camp"
19303 Fremont Ave. N.
Seattle, WA 98133
1-800-426-7010

2. Gather the necessary materials and publicize the event.

3. This activity requires the participants to fast. Ask them to secure parental permission.

Before the Activity

1. Ask the students how they would feel living in a Third World country. How do they feel entering into this awareness activity?

2. Divide into pairs and pray for each other. Ask God to instill an awareness of poor countries and what we can do to help their situation.

During the Activity

1. Proceed with the guidelines listed in the packet.

2. Allow one to two hours for discussion at the end of the activity.

Discussion

1. What weaknesses in your life did this exercise bring to light? strengths?

2. Why is it easy to overlook poor countries?

3. How can we use this new awareness in our lives? How can we make a difference?

4. Read Matthew 25:31-46; Mark 10:21. As Christians, what are we to do?

VISITING SHUT-INS

Time: one hour (preparation);
three and one-half hours (activity).
Group Size: three or more.

Description

The students will go out in groups of three to visit shut-ins for extended periods of time, talking with them, and assisting them in yard or household chores. The students will be stretched as they meet strangers and attempt to meet the needs of people with less physical ability.

Preparation

1. Obtain names from your pastor or the local senior service center of shut-ins who would appreciate a visit.

2. Make contact with each of the shut-ins and arrange an ap-

propriate time to visit. Ask how the group members may be of service to them (outdoor work, cleaning, shopping, etc.).

3. Collect materials you will need to do the jobs and arrange for transportation.

Before the Activity

1. Discuss what the youth imagine are the needs of shut-ins and how they can meet these needs.

2. Have each participant share his or her apprehensions about visiting the shut-ins.

3. Talk briefly with the students about situations they might expect to find among elderly shut-ins (loss of memory, poor hearing, unkept homes, etc.).

4. Have the participants develop some questions and topics to discuss with the shut-ins; for example, feelings such as loneliness, interests, past history, etc.

During the Activity

1. Divide the youth into groups of three. Drive to the homes and let the students help the elderly and talk with them.

2. Allow 30 minutes for discussion at the end of the activity.

Discussion

1. Have each person share about his or her experience, including what he or she was feeling during the visit.

2. How did the other two people you were with help you overcome your apprehensions? How did you support the others? Why did you need each other?

3. What did you learn about loneliness?

4. What did you learn about servanthood?

5. What do you want to remember from this experience?

6. How can you apply what you have learned to your everyday life?

VISITING THE HANDICAPPED

Time: 30 minutes (preparation); three hours (activity).
Group Size: six to 10.

Description

The students will spend time doing a recreational activity with handicapped individuals. The problems of attempting to communicate and relate with people who have physical and/or mental disabilities will challenge the group members to look beyond the external and view people as God might see them. This exercise will cause the participants to feel inadequate in their own abilities to communicate and relate and will compel them to seek help from their peers.

Preparation

1. Call the regional office of your state's Department of Social and Health Services and request the name of an organization in your area which is working with the handicapped and might appreciate a visit from your group.

2. Contact the agency to be visited. Obtain the following information from them:

- When is the best time to visit, and for how long?
- How many group members can you bring?
- What type of handicapped individuals reside at the facility?
- What should the students bring? wear?
- Any other knowledge the group members will need to know before visiting.

3. Arrange for transportation.

4. Gather any necessary equipment such as balls, books, paper, crayons, jump ropes, etc.

Before the Activity

1. Discuss with the students the difference between physically and mentally handicapped individuals:

- The group members will be able to relate to the physically handicapped as they normally would with people of that age. Communicating may be difficult if the residents are blind, deaf or have a speech impediment. The physically handicapped find their frustration in attempting to carry out physical tasks. The challenge for the participants working with them is to be creative in adapting the task and communication method to make both achievable.

- Mentally handicapped individuals must be related to at the level of ability which they possess. This is often similar to working with children. The mentally disabled tend to be very affectionate. The students will find it a challenge to relate with them.

2. Inform your group members that the key to working with the handicapped is to refrain from being overwhelmed by unusual behavior. Have them look beyond the person's behavior and see the individual God loves and created—an individual who may need a bit more love and attention than most people.

3. Prepare the participants to be ready to "jump right in" and get involved in the activities (no matter how insignificant they may seem). Decide which activities to do such as play catch,

swing on a swing set, walk around the block, jump rope, color pictures, etc.

4. Have each individual share his or her fears and apprehensions about this activity with the group.

5. Pray for one another.

During the Activity

1. Proceed to the area. Have the staff members give the students a brief orientation and introduce them to the handicapped individuals.

2. Allow 30 minutes for discussion at the end of the activity.

Discussion

1. Who was one particular person who made an impression upon you? How? Why?

2. What difficult situations did you encounter? How did you handle them? What did you learn from them?

3. When did you overcome your uncomfortable feelings? How did you do it?

4. How did this experience draw you closer to the members of your group?

5. How can you relate this experience to everyday life?

WHITEWATER RAFTING

Time: 30 minutes (preparation); five hours—depending on the distance to and from the site (activity).

Group Size: eight or more.

Description

The students will take a whitewater rafting trip. As participants experience the thrill of rushing rapids, they will become somewhat fearful for their safety. This need for support and encouragement from others, combined with the teamwork of paddling a raft together will bind the group members to one another.

Preparation

1. Contact a professional whitewater rafting guide service. It is important to find guides who have a good reputation and have passed stringent certification standards. A certified guide should be in every raft. The rafting company must have adequate liability insurance.

2. Request to raft a river rated at Class III (with a few Class IV rapids) for high school students and above.

3. Discuss your goals for the activity with your guides. Let them

know your desire to emphasize teamwork.

4. Rafters should wear swimsuits, sunglasses, old shoes and a lifejacket. On colder rivers you may be requested by the guide service to wear wetsuits or wool socks.

5. Instruct the participants to take an extra set of clothes to change into when they get off the river.

6. Each minor will be required to have a release form signed by his or her parent or guardian.

7. Choose a few bond building exercises (Chapter 2).

8. Arrange for transportation to and from the site. If you are a long distance from the site and camping is necessary, bring supplies, equipment and food.

Before the Activity

1. Have each person share with the group any apprehensions he or she has about whitewater rafting. This is important. Whitewater rafting causes a good deal of apprehension in some people yet very little in others. The sensitivity, or lack thereof, of the individual participants to the feelings of the other group members will become apparent at this point.

2. Divide into pairs and pray.

3. Instruct the participants to keep an eye open for things they might be able to learn as a result of rafting.

During the Activity

1. While on shore immediately prior to the event, play a few bond building exercises to establish the idea of teamwork in the minds of the group members.

2. Before asking the group members the discussion questions, allow them to change into dry clothes and drink something cold (or hot, depending upon the weather). Allow 30 minutes for discussion at the end of the activity.

Discussion

1. What were the highlights of the trip for you?

2. At what moment were you the most afraid? Why?

3. How did this group help you physically on the river?

4. How did being with this group help you deal with your fears? How did you help members of this group cope with their fears?

5. What did you learn about working together as a team which can be related to the group in everyday life?

6. Compare rafting with a guide to your relationship with God. What are similarities? differences?

CHAPTER 6:
DEEPER SHARING AND GOAL SETTING

If you have read the previous chapters and participated in the exercises, you are making progress in building community in your youth group. The participants moved through the first step with the bond building exercises. They "opened up" in the second step. Group members became more comfortable affirming one another at the third step. And the youth group members had a scary but fun time as they stretched in the fourth step.

Your "collection of individuals" is more solidified. Your group members actually care for one another and enjoy being around one another. They are willing to share their joys and their sorrows, victories and defeats.

Now it is time to move to the final step: deeper sharing and goal setting. Having developed a trust and care for one another through the first four steps of building community, the students are much more willing and able to let the group become the setting for true fellowship.

But for true fellowship to occur, individuals must feel comfortable and willing to share on a deeper level. Individuals must feel accepted, appreciated, and loved in order to share their *deepest* joys and *most intense* struggles, and to work with the group in becoming *all* that God wants them to be. They need a place that is free from ridicule and gossip. You have helped to create that place by incorporating the first four steps of building community in your youth group program.

Most students have areas in their lives they are anxious to improve. As they share deeply about their lives, they become more open to challenge themselves, to change or accept the

challenges of others. The group can assist an individual by listening to what the person shares, and by talking through options and
methods of change. People can deal effectively with a problem,
only through verbalization of the problem and its potential solutions. The first step toward healing is the admission of the problem. Then students can offer one another low-level accountability
and high-level support in the pursuit of the goal and at the same
time give each other the freedom to fail.

As the students encounter everyday struggles, they need to be
able to turn to one another for emotional support and encouragement. Getting "dumped" by a girlfriend, being laughed at for
abstaining from alcohol and drugs, being cut from the volleyball
team, struggling with sexual temptation or enduring a tough situation at home may seem like manageable problems to adults. But
they are massive problems to teenagers. (Remember your own
adolescence?) They weigh heavily and demand support.

This chapter contains 23 deeper sharing and goal setting exercises which promote an atmosphere of encouragement and support
for you and your group. These programmed activities allow
students to verbalize their perceptions about current struggles and
victories in their lives. Where opening up exercises focused
primarily upon the *past* (personal history), deeper sharing and
goal setting exercises emphasize the present and the future.

Most of the exercises in this chapter provide an opportunity for
students to set goals to improve their lives. Care must be taken to
ensure that group members feel the freedom to fail in the accomplishment of these goals. Goals are merely targets and
guidelines for growth; they do not exist to produce guilt.

How to Use the Deeper Sharing and Goal Setting Exercises

1. *Work on goals that are both measurable and achievable.* "I
will personally share my faith with every student in the school" is
measurable but probably not achievable. It is also a goal that pro-
duces a tremendous amount of guilt. A more realistic and effective
goal would be, "I will share my faith with one of my friends this
month."

2. *Gently remind students which struggles are appropriate to
discuss with the total group.* Problems which involve the negative
behavioral traits of other group members need not be shared with
the whole group. For example, "I'm trying to be patient when
Debbie gets possessive of our friendship." Group discussions
should abstain from intimate subjects and from becoming an open
arena for gripes about the school system, parents, etc. These subjects are dealt with more effectively one-on-one.

3. *Ask the students to write down their goals.* Goals are more easily recalled when written. They also can be placed in a prominent spot at home for a daily reminder.

4. *Encourage the group to actively listen to one another.* It is extremely threatening for young people to tell one another about present struggles and joys. The group members must show they care. If necessary, review the listening skills in the opening up exercises in Chapter 3.

5. *Model openness as the leader.* Students will only share as deeply as you do. Talk about some of your goals. Ask them to hold you accountable; and ask them to reciprocate to you the freedom to fail.

6. *Utilize teachable moments.* In this final stage of building community, the students are much more open in their level of sharing. They feel comfortable with you and with one another. Capitalize on teachable moment topics such as leadership, cooperation, frustration, resourcefulness, etc.

The given discussion questions focus on teachable moments and allow for deeper probing of feelings. Feel free to adapt the questions or add your own.

With these guidelines in mind, let's proceed with the exercises.

ALL ABOARD

Time: one hour.
Materials: a handout and pencil for each person.

Description

1. Distribute a pencil and a copy of the handout on the following page to each person.

Discussion

1. Gather together and have each person share his or her answers to the first three questions on the handout. Have the group members confirm whether or not they agree with each individual's answer to the third question.

2. Finish by having each person share his or her answers to the last questions.

Variations

1. In the first question, substitute "in our youth group" for "in my school."

2. In the first question, substitute "in my family" for "in my school."

1. If this cartoon represented the people in my school, I would (circle the person).
2. Why did you choose the person?
3. Who in the picture do you think others perceive you as being? Why do you think they characterize you in this way?
4. Who in the picture would you like to be? Why do you want to be that type of person?
5. How do you think you might be able to become this type of person?

AMOEBA

Time: 20 minutes.

Materials: 30-foot piece of cord. Plot a course around the meeting area. Include at least one stairway.

Description

1. Have the group stand as close together as possible.
2. Tie the cord tightly around the group.
3. Have the members take a walk over a designated course.

Discussion

1. To what extent did you feel like you were working together as a group?
2. Did you feel like you were in control of where you were going? Explain.
3. Who emerged as the leader(s)? How were they selected?
4. Did this exercise hurt at all? Why or why not?
5. What would have happened if one person in the front or back had suddenly stopped?
6. How is this exercise similar to the functioning of the body of

Christ as referred to in Romans 12:4-8 and 1 Corinthians 12:12-27.

7. What is the key to the successful accomplishment of this exercise?

Variation

If the group members had trouble with Amoeba, after answering the above questions, have them try the exercise once more. Then ask the following questions:

• How were the results of this exercise different the second time from the first time?

• What did you learn from this experience that you can apply to our group on a continual basis?

DUAL PERSONALITY

Time: 40 minutes.

Materials: a paper and pencil for each person.

Description/Discussion

1. Distribute a paper and pencil to each person.

2. Give the youth five minutes to be as specific as possible in writing the answers to the following questions:

• List five ways you are prone to act when you're feeling good about yourself.

• List five ways you are prone to act when you're feeling poorly about yourself.

3. Go around the group and have each person share three of his or her answers to each question.

4. Next give the youth five minutes to be as specific as possible in writing the answers to the following questions:

• List five things that encourage you to feel good about yourself.

• List five things that encourage you to feel poorly about yourself.

5. Go around the group and allow individuals to share three of their answers to each question.

6. Ask each person to answer the following question: "What specific changes can you make in your life this week to help you feel better about yourself?"

7. Organize into groups of three and allow each person to share the changes he or she will do this week to make him or her feel better.

FACES OF ME

Time: 45 minutes.

Materials: one copy of the poem "Faces of Me" by Verne Becker for each person.

Description

1. Distribute the copies of the following poem "Faces of Me" by Verne Becker. Have the students read the poem.

FACES OF ME

I am not really myself.
I am someone else.
When others see me to talk to me
They are talking to a stranger,
Not me.
I am kept hidden away,
Safe from discovery or attack,
Behind the cover of my masks.
Each day.
Sometimes knowingly, sometimes not.
As I sift through my closet,
Choosing which clothes to wear,
I also search my mental mask menagerie,
Carefully selecting the image I want to project.

Like an actor,
I have learned to portray many roles,
Many faces,
Many moods.
And I use a different mask for each.
Each mask represents something about me,
The me I would like to be.
I put on a mask of happiness because
I sincerely want to be happy,
I wear the socialite mask because
I want friends to have fun with,
The self-sufficiency mask because
I truly want to take charge of my life.
I know these goals are worthwhile.
And I view the masks as a way
To help me reach those goals
By putting my best foot forward.

Something peculiar happens, however,
As I continue wearing these masks.
They begin to feel too comfortable.
Natural.

Necessary.
I can go for weeks without removing them.
As if they were extended-wear contact lenses
That only require an occasional cleaning.
As I get used to my masks,
I begin to believe they might really be me
Rather than merely a facade.
Yet meanwhile,
My true self lies dormant with me.
Isolated.
Forgotten.

So rather than bringing me closer to my goals,
The masks alienate me from them.
Like a brick wall, the masks confine me.
Isolate me.
Hide me from other people.
And before long I realize
I'm not what my mask says I am,
But exactly the opposite.
When I don the mask of conformity,
Identifying me with a certain group,
I'm really broadcasting my own lack of identity,
My own uncertainty of who I am.
Or when I wear the mask of confidence,
Refusing to admit weakness, mistakes or hurt,
I'm telegraphing my own insecurity.

I have other masks that I maintain
For use at the proper time:
The mask of superiority
To stare down inferior feelings
I detect in others
And in myself;
The mask of appearance
To enhance my attractiveness to others
So I'll forget how ugly I think I am;
The clown or the rowdy masks
To gain the attention I can't obtain otherwise;
The "totally together" mask
To hide all my rough edges;
The mask of love
To disguise an overly selfish relationship;
Even the mask of spirituality

To silence all questions about my status before
    God.

What should I do with all these masks?
I realize they have insulated me
Not only from other people.
But also from myself.
If indeed I want to be myself
Rather than someone else.
I must remove the masks,
Peel them off,
Cut them away like a plaster cast.
Some of the worthless masks I will trample to pieces.
Others I will display on my bedroom wall
To remind me of the person I'd like to be,
But am not yet.

I can openly walk toward the goals
Those good masks represent,
Because being real doesn't mean giving up
On areas I need to change.
Nor does it mean I'm satisfied
With everything about myself.
It simply means accepting the way I am now,
And honestly admitting
I'm still working on my problems.

Ultimately, I won't need masks;
Instead,
I'll show others the living person behind them:
Not a stranger, but
A special, unique,
Authentic human being—
Someone who's not perfect, but who wants to grow.
Only when I open myself to other people
Will I see myself clearly.
And only when I take off the masks
Will I be truly free.

---

2. Ask each person the following questions. Make sure each individual answers questions 1, 2 and 6.

Discussion

1. In what specific ways does this poem describe your life?
2. What masks do you have a tendency to hide behind?
3. Why do your masks feel nice and secure to you?
4. What does being "real" mean?
5. After reading and discussing this poem, to what extent do you want to take off your masks? Why?
6. What specific things can you do this week to begin removing your masks?

FAMILY FEUD

Time: 45 minutes.
Materials: none.

Description

1. Instruct the students to close their eyes and imagine the following scenario. When you read the material, pause at each ellipsis (...) to give the youth a chance to picture the scene.

"Visualize yourself walking into your house at about supper time ... You close the door and walk into the kitchen ... Your parents are in the kitchen, and you can tell that they are angry with you ... Imagine what their body posture is like ... What facial expressions do they have? ... What are each of them saying? ... How are they saying it? ...

"Now imagine yourself responding to your parents ... What do you say to them? ... How do you say it? ... What is your body posture? ... What are your facial expressions? ... How does this communication between you and your parents end? ... What feelings do you have toward your parents after it is over? ... What feelings do they have toward you?...

"Keep your eyes closed. How could your communication with your parents be improved by *you*? ... What could you do differently to improve your relationship with them? ..."
2. Have the students open their eyes.

Discussion

1. What is your personalized view of the scenario?
2. How can you improve your communication with your parents?
3. What could you do differently to improve your communication with them? (It is important that the youth focus on what *they* can do to help the situation rather than on the problems they perceive their parents to have.)

FRIENDS FOREVER

Time: 35 minutes.
Materials: a paper and pencil for each person.

Description/Discussion

1. Instruct the group members to think about two specific moments in their lives when they have felt extremely close to one or more people.

2. Have them describe these experiences to the group. What was the main reason these moments were so special?

3. Allow the other group members to ask questions about the experiences.

4. Distribute the paper and pencils. Have the participants individually write down:

• What could you do in your current friendships to make them closer?

• What is one thing you will do this week to promote a closer friendship with someone? (Be specific.)

5. Discuss the answers.

GROUP RATE

Time: 30 minutes.
Materials: a pencil and Group Evaluation Form for each person.

Description

1. Distribute a pencil and the following evaluation to each person. Give the youth 10 minutes to fill it out.

GROUP EVALUATION FORM

Place a number (1-5) in each blank, rating this group according to the percentage of the time you feel the group displays the listed characteristics. Your responses will be kept anonymous.

    1 = 100 percent
    2 = 75 percent
    3 = 50 percent
    4 = 25 percent
    5 =   0 percent

The youth group members:

_____ understand the things I try to say.

_____ cooperate and work well together.

_____ care more about themselves than the task at hand.

_____ trust each other with their feelings.

_____ communicate well.

> _____ are overly concerned about what the other people in the group think.
> _____ can accomplish what they set out to do.
> _____ do not interrupt me or ignore my comments.
> _____ accept me as I am.
> _____ let me know exactly what they think of me.
> _____ care about me and my needs.
> _____ include me in "what's happening."
> _____ respect my ideas and thoughts.
> _____ enjoy my presence.

2. Collect all of the evaluations and tabulate the results. Discuss the results, including where the group scored the highest and lowest.

Discussion

1. What has this exercise taught you about this group?
2. Are there any changes you would like to see made in this group?

THE IDEAL LIFE

Time: 25 minutes.
Materials: a pencil and handout for each person.

Description

1. Distribute a pencil and the following handout to each person.

> 1. What changes would you have to make in the following areas for you to feel you are living an "ideal" life?
> - personal
> - family
> - school
> - community
> - spiritual
> 2. What are two specific steps you will take during the next 24 hours to make some of these changes a reality?

2. Give the group members 10 minutes to write out their answers.

Discussion

1. Ask each person to explain a couple of his or her answers.
2. Allow the others to ask questions to clarify answers or draw out each individual.

I'M OKAY

Time: 35 minutes.
Materials: a handout and pencil for each person.

Description

1. Distribute a pencil and the following handout to each person.

---

1. List as many aspects as you can think of which you don't like about yourself.

2. Place check marks by those which worry you the most.

3. Of these, cross out the ones you really can't do anything about.

4. Circle the one aspect you are willing to actually sacrifice money, time or effort to change.

5. Star the one you want to concentrate on this next month.

6. List five things you can do this next month to change the one aspect.

7. Of those five, circle the one you'll do tomorrow.

---

2. Give the group members 10 minutes to complete the handout.

Discussion

1. Ask each individual to share his or her answers to the fourth, fifth and seventh questions.
2. Allow the others to ask questions to clarify answers or draw out each individual.

I NEED

Time: 20 minutes.
Materials: a 3x5 card and pencil for each person.

Description

1. Distribute a pencil and 3x5 card to each person.
2. Have the group members write out their answers to the following questions:
   • In this group, I need from the leaders ...
   • In this group, I need from the members ...
   • In this group, I need from myself ...

3. Collect the cards, shuffle and redistribute them.

Discussion

1. State that the goal of this exercise is for everyone to understand the expectations of the group members a bit better. Have each person read the card he or she is holding.

2. Allow the group members to make additional comments.

Variation

Using the same format, substitute "I expect" for "I need."

LIFE

Time: 40 minutes.
Materials: a paper and pencil for each person.

Description

1. Distribute a paper and pencil to each person.

2. Give the group members 10 minutes to answer the following questions:
   • List five things which make life meaningful for you.
   • List five things in life that make you want to crawl into bed, pull the covers over your head and never come out.

Discussion

1. Ask each individual to share his or her answers.

2. Allow the others to ask questions to clarify answers.

THE OUTSIDERS

Time: 15 minutes.
Materials: none.

Description

1. Pick one or two people to be the "outsiders."

2. Have the remaining members of the group stand in a circle close together. The people forming the circle are supposed to try to keep the "outsiders" from getting inside the circle.

3. Instruct the "outsiders" to try and get inside the circle. This is a physical activity, so be careful. Make sure the activity doesn't get out of hand. If one person struggles, but can't get inside, give someone else a try.

4. Let each person have the opportunity to be an "outsider." Stop the activity early if the momentum begins to slow down (when people quit trying or they get the point of the exercise).

Discussion

1. How did you react to being an "outsider"?

2. How did it feel to try keeping the "outsiders" from gaining entry into the group?

3. How do you usually treat people who are newcomers to this group?

4. What subtle "initiation process" are newcomers put through before they are allowed to be an accepted part of the group?

5. Upon what do we base our acceptance of others into this group?

6. What did you learn about yourself from this experience?

7. Based upon what we have learned, how could we as a group change for the better?

OVERCOMING ADVERSITY

Time: 45 minutes.

Materials: a handout and pencil for each person.

Description

1. Distribute a pencil and the following handout to each person.

Think of two problems you are currently dealing with in your life. Answer the following questions about them in the space provided.

Problem	**People and situations I blame for causing this problem**
1.	1.
2.	2.

How I contribute to causing this problem	**What I can do to make the situation better**
1.	1.
2.	2.

What I could do which would make the situation worse

1.

2.

---

2. Give the group members 10 minutes to complete the handout.

Discussion

1. Gather in a circle and have each person share one of his or her answers.

2. Allow the others to ask questions to clarify answers or to draw out each individual.

OVER THE HILL

Time: 40 minutes.
Materials: a handout and pencil for each person.

Description

1. Distribute a pencil and the following handout to each person.

---

1. What do you want your life to be like when you are 40? Focus on character qualities, hobbies, career, lifestyle, etc.

2. Why are these characteristics important to you?

3. What can you do now to begin reaching these goals?

4. How can this group help you?

---

2. Give each student five minutes to complete the handout.

Discussion

1. Gather in a circle and have each person share his or her answers.
2. Allow the others to ask questions to clarify answers or to draw out each individual.

PERCEPTIONS

Time: 50 minutes.
Materials: a handout and pencil for each person.

Description

1. Distribute a pencil and the following handout to each person.

---

1. How would your parents describe you? Focus on characteristics, attitudes, beliefs, temperament, etc.

2. How would your best friend describe you?

3. How would your teacher describe you?

4. How would you describe you?

5. Why do some people see you differently?

6. Do you feel this is good or bad? Why?

---

2. Give each student 15 minutes to complete the handout. Encourage the youth to think deeply and write in detail.

Discussion

1. Gather in a circle and have each student share his or her answers.
2. Allow the others to ask clarifying questions.

SINGIN' THE BLUES

Time: 45 minutes.
Materials: a pencil and handout for each person.

Description

1. Distribute the following handout and a pencil to each person.

> 1. Write down a time you felt lonely:
> • in grade school
> • in junior high
> • within the past year
> • within the past month
> 2. How have times of loneliness added depth to your life?
> 3. What has helped you overcome loneliness?
> 4. What have you done to help people who are lonely?

2. Allow the group members 10 minutes to write out their answers to the questions on the handout.

Discussion

1. Gather in a circle.
2. Go around the room, one question at a time, and have everyone share his or her answers.

SQUARES

Time: one hour.
Materials: one set of square parts per group (see step 1).

Description

1. Make a set of squares for each group of five to seven people. Follow these directions:

A set consists of five envelopes containing pieces of cardboard cut into different patterns which (when properly arranged) will form five squares of equal size. One set should be provided for each group of five persons.

To prepare a set, cut out five cardboard squares, each exactly

6x6. Place the squares in a row and mark them as below, penciling the letters lightly so they can be erased.

The lines should be so drawn that, when the pieces are cut out, those marked A will be exactly the same size, all pieces marked C the same size, etc. Several combinations are possible that will form one or two squares, but only one combination will form all five squares, each 6x6. After drawing the lines on the squares and labeling the sections with letters, cut each square along the lines into smaller pieces to make the parts of the puzzle.

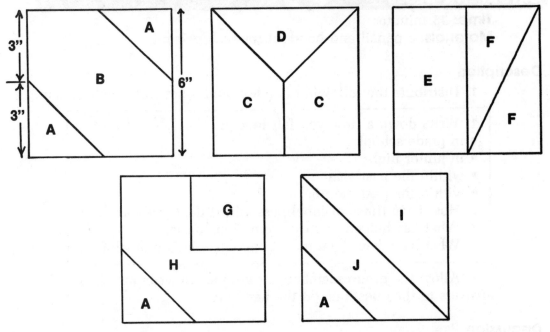

Label the five envelopes 1, 2, 3, 4 and 5. Distribute the cardboard pieces into the five envelopes as follows: envelope 1 has pieces I, H, E; 2 has A, A, A, C; 3 has A, J; 4 has D, F; and 5 has G, B, F, C.

Erase the penciled letter from each piece and write, instead, the number of the envelope it is in. This makes it easy to return the pieces to the proper envelope, for subsequent use, after a group has completed the task.

2. Participants in this exercise are put in a situation where they are forced to learn the benefits of giving to others. The sets of squares are broken down in such a way that one person may, after completing his or her square, need to break that square up in order for all the group members' squares to come together. Sometimes all of the participants hand their pieces over to one group member for him or her to put together—only to find that they could actually have put the squares together better by themselves.

These situations cause frustrations, as the other participants are unable to take pieces of squares when they want them.

3. Divide into groups of five to seven people.

4. Give each group a set of square parts. Give five of the participants in each group an envelope.

5. Instruct the participants who do not have envelopes to be observers. They are to watch and make mental notes about the group's interaction.

6. Give the people with envelopes these rules:

• They may not communicate with one another—verbally or nonverbally.

• They each must put together a square.

• They may not take a square piece from another individual.

• The task is completed when all five squares in the group are put together.

• Pieces may not be set in the middle for just anyone to take. They must be given to a specific individual.

7. Tell the participants to complete the square-building task as quickly as possible. Don't give a specific time limit, but periodically tell them to hurry and finish.

Discussion

1. How did you feel as you worked on this project? frustrated? anxious? Explain.

2. Could you have done anything different to complete the task more quickly?

3. Have each designated "observer" share his or her observations.

4. What was the key to "solving" this problem?

5. Who initially was willing to give away his or her pieces?

6. How does this exercise relate to Mark 8:35 and John 12:24?

7. Is the giving or lack of giving which you displayed in this exercise in any way typical of yourself in other situations?

8. As a result of this exercise, what is one thing you learned about yourself?

SUCCESS AND FAILURE

Time: 30 minutes.

Materials: a Bible for each person.

Description

1. Gather the participants in a circle, then distribute the Bibles.

2. Ask the following questions:

Discussion

1. What do you view in life as some of your "big" successes? What made them successes?

2. What do you view in life as some of your "big" failures? What make them failures?

3. Ask the youth to read aloud the following verses: 1 Samuel 15:22; 1 Chronicles 22:13; Psalm 51:16-17; Proverbs 1:1-7; Hosea 6:6; Matthew 7:24-27; Luke 14:28-30; 1 Corinthians 13; Hebrews 11:32-40.

4. How does God define success? failure?

5. What implications does this discussion have on your life in this group? with your family? at school? in sports?

TEN STEPS TO A BETTER FAMILY

Time: 20 minutes.
Materials: a paper and pencil for each person.

Description

1. Distribute the paper and pencils.

2. Read the "10 Steps" to the participants and give them 10 minutes to complete their answers.

---

10 STEPS

- List seven problems your family has.
- Circle three to which *you* contribute.
- Rewrite and expand one of these.
- List five specific things which can be done to alleviate the problem.
- Underline two you could do.
- Circle one you *will* do.
- What are four things which could *hinder* you from actually doing this?
- What are four things which will *help* you to actually do this?
- When will you do it?
- How can the group help you accomplish this?

Discussion

1. Have each person share his or her answers to questions 2, 6, 9 and 10 of the "10 Steps."

2. After a person shares, have a time of prayer for him or her before hearing from the next participant.

UNITED WE STAND, DIVIDED WE FALL

Time: two hours.

Materials: a Ranking Sheet, Role Nomination handout and pencil for each person.

Description

1. Distribute the pencils and the Ranking Sheets.

2. Have the participants individually rank the biggest problems facing teenagers in your community.

3. After everyone is finished, have the participants rank the problems by reaching a consensus as a group. (Do not allow group sponsors to talk during this time.)

Ranking Sheet

Individual Rank	Group Rank	
————	————	Dealing with peer pressure
————	————	Drug abuse
————	————	Dealing with loneliness
————	————	Making financial ends meet
————	————	Completing academic studies
————	————	Dealing with family problems
————	————	Alcohol abuse
————	————	Finding peace of mind
————	————	Deciding who God is
————	————	Time management
————	————	Finding and keeping quality friends
————	————	Making plans for the future
————	————	Deciding how to relate sexually
————	————	Dealing with feelings of low self-worth
————	————	Other

---

4. Distribute the Role Nomination handout. Have each person decide what roles the individual members of the group (including himself or herself) portrayed during this exercise. When done, share these with the group.

Role Nomination

Nominate each person in the group for one of the following roles (include yourself). Do not give any individual more than one role.

Name	Role
_____	1. Data processor: brain; analyzes and organizes information

---

_____	2. Fireman: puts out fires
_____	3. Principal: oversees and coordinates
_____	4. Minister: cares and encourages
_____	5. Doctor: gets to the heart of the matter
_____	6. Telephone repairman: keeps the lines open
_____	7. Entertainer: relieves tension
_____	8. Trucker: keeps things moving
_____	9. Junk collector: takes other people's ideas, recycles them and turns them into gold
_____	10. Printer: finalizes and records ideas
_____	11. Electrician: energizes and motivates
_____	12. Psychologist: listens intently

Discussion

1. How did you feel about how the group sought a consensus? Why?

2. What are your reactions to the roles for which the group nominated you? How did they differ from the role in which you placed yourself?

3. To what extent do you feel your behavior in this exercise is typical of your normal behavior in this group?

4. What did you learn about this group through this exercise?

THE WALL

Time: 45 minutes.

Materials: a paper and pencil for each person.

Description

1. Paint the following scenario in the minds of the group members: "Visualize yourself walking along a peaceful, tranquil path ... The pathway leads to God ... Suddenly your progress is blocked entirely by a wall ... This wall is inhibiting you from getting closer to God."

2. Distribute paper and pencils. Ask the youth to answer the following questions on paper:

• Describe what this wall represents in your life. How did it get there? How hard have you tried to overcome or tear down this wall in the past?

• How best can this wall be overcome? (Be as specific as possible.)

• What is one thing you will commit yourself to do this week to eliminate this wall?

• How can the group help you accomplish this?

Discussion

1. Ask each person to share his or her answers.
2. Allow others to ask clarifying questions.
3. Close in prayer for each other's goals for the coming week.

WEEK IN REVIEW

Time: 45 minutes.

Materials: a pencil and several 3x5 cards for each person.

Description/Discussion

1. Go around the room and have each student share answers to the following questions:

• What was the highlight of this past week for you?

• What was the worst thing that happened to you this past week?

• What were the best and worst interactions that happened this past week between you and your father? mother? teacher? friend?

• What are two apprehensions you have about this upcoming week?

2. Distribute the 3x5 cards and pencils.

3. Have each student write a note of encouragement to each of the people about whom he or she shared. Ask the youth to mail the notes this week.

WHO ARE YOU?

Time: 40 minutes.

Materials: a handout and pencil for each person.

Description

1. Distribute the following handout and a pencil to each person. Give each person 10 minutes to complete the handout.

In the blanks, please rate how true each of the following statements is for you.

1 = always 2 = typically 3 = sometimes
4 = seldom 5 = rarely 6 = never

_____ like being mellow

_____ want to be with people all the time

_____ let other people decide what we do

_____ want to have close, personal relationships with others

_____ want to be included in everything the group does
_____ let other people do the initiating in relationships
_____ try to control other people
_____ am sought out by others
_____ like being vulnerable with others
_____ want others to be honest with me
_____ need to be by myself once in a while
_____ like being questioned about how I'm doing
_____ like to listen more than talk
_____ interrupt others
_____ am easy to get to know and understand
_____ don't trust others until I've tested them
_____ listen well to people's problems
_____ try to impress others
_____ feel uncomfortable with those I don't know
_____ have a sarcastic, teasing sense of humor
_____ don't let other people know how much I care about them
_____ give of my time and money to others
_____ get annoyed easily at others
_____ often feel rejected by others
_____ expect the best from others
_____ like to give my opinion on everything
_____ give compliments to others frequently

2. Clear an area in the room and designate a contingency line going from 1 to 6. Read each question aloud and have the participants place themselves on the line according to their answers.

Discussion

1. What did you enjoy about this exercise?
2. What made this exercise difficult?
3. What did you learn about yourself by doing this exercise?
4. What is one thing about yourself you would like to improve?
5. What is one thing about yourself you would like to stay the same?

CHAPTER 7:
MEETINGS

Chapters 2 through 6 gave you all the ideas, guidelines and exercises you need to start building community in your youth group. This chapter incorporates the previous information and gives you two formats to use with your group to build community.

The first format is for one month: four week night meetings and one Saturday event to take your group from the first step through the fifth step in building community.

The second format is a detailed description of an all-day event to take your students through the group building process.

You could plan one of these formats for your group or you could plan both and really cement your group together. It's totally up to you!

ONE-MONTH FORMAT

One way to build community with your youth is to concentrate for one month on the theme of group building. Spend four night meetings and one Saturday on the process. During this period you'll move through the bond building exercises to the deeper sharing and goal setting exercises. Your group will become a community and a force to be reckoned with in the kingdom. Here's the plan for the one-month format:

Week One

The purposes for the first week are: to help the students get to know each other on a first-name basis; to work as a team in close proximity; to talk about what they learned; to share a little more about themselves. All of this takes place in a fun, casual, relaxed atmosphere. The progression of the exercises helps to create this atmosphere.

The meeting begins with a name game, moves through three bond building exercises, includes a debriefing time and concludes with one opening up activity. The exercises have been designed at a low vulnerability level.

Also included in the exercises are sample instructions and directions for you to say to your students. Feel free to alter the directions and use your own words.

When you introduce the exercises, use the name of the step they're from: bond building, opening up, affirming, stretching, and deeper sharing and goal setting. Explain to the students the purpose of each step. By doing so, you are helping the students understand the strategy, terms and purpose of group building— skills they will need later when they serve as youth leaders or sponsors.

Before you begin, read the guidelines in Chapters 2 and 3 on how most effectively to lead bond building and opening up exercises.

Begin the meeting by saying: "In the next month, we are going to move through a five-step process that will help us better understand ourselves, each other and God. The month may seem slightly different from what you may have experienced previously because we're going to have lots of participation, some discussion and zero lecture. You'll see how it develops as we move along.

"Right now, we're going to get to know one another by name by playing Name Game. Let's get in a circle. I'll start by giving my name, 'Hi, I'm Denny,' and the next person will say my name and then his own name, 'He's Denny and I'm Ryan.' We will move around the circle and repeat everyone's name."

Play Name Game and, as the leader, enjoy it. Convey the idea that you're having a good time.

Then say: "Now that we know everyone's name, let's do a little bond building exercise called Knots." Explain the concept of bond building and follow the directions on page 41. Include the discussion questions but don't spend too much time on them. Do not do the teachable moment questions in the designated box. These are for a later time when community has been built in the group and the members are willing to share deeper feelings. Right now, the emphasis is on building bonds, getting to know each other and having fun.

Continue by saying: "Okay, I've got another bond building activity. This one is called Blind Line Up and requires a little creativity and teamwork." Follow the directions on page 34. After you've played the game, move through the discussion questions.

Then say: "All right, you've proved yourselves. Now we're ready for something really difficult." Introduce Climbing the Walls (page 36). If you have 12 or more students, divide into two teams. When you've completed the exercise, have the group sit in a circle and talk through the discussion questions.

Then ask the participants to focus on these questions to evaluate the previous activities.

1. What was the most difficult part of these exercises for you?
2. What did you see as the purpose for doing them?
3. How well did the group solve the problems presented?
4. What else did you learn from them?

Finally say: "We've learned each other's names and we've worked together as a team. As we conclude tonight, I'd like all of us to get to know each other a little better." Introduce the youth to the opening up activity Three Minutes (page 71). Discuss the concept of "opening up." If your group members haven't done much speaking in front of each other, only give them one minute to speak. As the leader, set the stage by sharing about yourself.

Wrap up the evening by reviewing what the participants have done, what they've learned (summarize the answers to the debriefing questions) and encourage them to come next week. The youth will be encouraged to come by the fun they had and by the fact that a group of their peers really listened to them when they shared.

Week Two

In this meeting, you'll move to one more stage than you did in the first week. By the conclusion of this meeting, you and the group will be at the third step in building community—Affirming. (Read through the guidelines in Chapter 4 on how most effectively to lead the affirming exercises.)

To bring the group to this stage, you'll do three bond building exercises, one more opening up activity and two affirming exercises. By the end of the session, the students will feel like they know each other better and they will have begun to appreciate one another.

Welcome everyone to the meeting. Begin by saying: "Last week we began a month-long series on group building. We participated in a few exercises that gave us some insights about each other and helped to build bonds. We're going to continue with three bond building activities."

Introduce the bond building exercise Lap Sit (page 42). Move through that exercise fairly quickly and include the discussion questions. Then do Stand Up (page 52). Again, move through this fairly quickly and include the discussion questions. These bond building exercises are simply to reinforce the bond building that went on in the first week and to help newcomers feel a part of the total group.

Continue with another bond building exercise Radioactive Swamp (page 48). Introduce it by saying: "Now we're going to move to an activity that will tax some of your problem-solving abilities. It's called the Radioactive Swamp." Explain the directions to the group members and let them play. Go through the questions in the discussion.

Next say: "Okay. We've learned a little bit about group process and solidified some bonds between us. Now we're going to open up and take a look at ourselves. We're going to do that through an activity called Forced Choice." Follow the directions on page 62. Move through the activity and include the discussion questions.

Now you're ready to move to the third step in building community—affirming. To do that, explain this step of the process to the youth and make this transition: "I really appreciate you taking the time to be honest during Forced Choice. I know that I personally appreciated the honesty of … (give a few examples of what you've learned and what you appreciate). Now let's take a few minutes to appreciate and affirm one another by writing a few telegrams."
Give the participants the directions for Telegrams (page 89). If you have a very large group, divide into groups of 10 for this exercise.

Conclude with a Group Hug (page 87). This affirming exercise is a short, fun way to say thanks to each other.

Announce and discuss the special all-day Saturday event. In preparation for this, you will need to choose and set up one of the stretching exercises listed in Chapter 5 such as Rock Climbing, Community Service, Visiting the Handicapped, Prison Visit, etc. Read the guidelines in Chapter 5 on how most effectively to lead stretching exercises.

Week Two: Saturday

This is a special day. After two weeks of working through the community building process, you'll have a full day to be with the troops and grow together. You'll open with a bond building activity, bounce to an affirming exercise, then go on to level four—stretching!

Serve sweet rolls and orange juice as the group arrives. Welcome them warmly (morning comes early for some of these people)!

Review where the group has been in the month-long process so far. Say: "By the time we're done today, we will have stretched a bit and continued to learn more about ourselves, our world and our God.

"We're going to begin with another bond building activity that can teach us a lot. It's called the Trust Fall." See page 53 and give the directions to the group. When you come to the discussion time, use the discussion questions *and* the teachable moment questions in the designated box. In this instance, the Trust Fall is more than a bond building exercise. The students have built bonds, opened up and are ready to share deeper feelings.

After the Trust Fall, play the affirming exercise Names in a Hat (page 88). Introduce it by saying: "Before we participate in our stretching experience, I want to give us a chance to do a little affirmation exercise called Names in a Hat. It goes like this ..." (Give the instructions.)

Now you're ready to stretch. Explain the purpose of this step in the process of building community. Introduce the experience by saying: "As I mentioned to you last week, we've got a great activity planned that I think will stretch us. It's called ... (give the name of the activity)." Brief the group members on the activity. Without going into too much detail, tell them what to expect. Ask them what apprehensions they might have for doing this activity, what they're looking forward to, etc. Then do the activity you've selected from the stretching exercises. Be sure to leave time for debriefing afterward. Go through the discussion questions and allow time for the students to share what they've learned from the event.

Announce that the next meeting will last from 4 to 8 p.m. and ask all youth to arrive on time (but don't give them any more details). Advance notice on this upcoming stretching exercise will diminish the learning experience. Only you and a couple other trusted confidants—all sworn to absolute secrecy—should know.

Week Three

Tonight you are going to spend four hours playing a stretching exercise called Hard Bargain. It is an exercise that can lead to great frustration and great teaching, but it will stretch the group.

In advance, read over the instructions for Hard Bargain (page 99). Run the meeting according to those instructions and make sure you give enough time for debriefing through the discussion questions. This will be a great night that few students will forget.

By the time the night is over, your group members will have spent three weeks in the community building process and will have moved through four steps—bond building, opening up, affirming and stretching. You're ready to move to the fifth step—deeper sharing and goal setting.

Week Four

This is the last week of the monthly series on group building. In this final meeting, you and the group will do two deeper sharing and goal setting activities and you will end with an affirming exercise. By the end of the meeting, you will have moved through all five steps and will have experienced first-hand the group building process. Your group members will be much more cohesive and excited about themselves, each other and God. Before you begin, read the guidelines in Chapter 6 on how most effectively to lead deeper sharing and goal setting exercises.

Welcome the group members. Thank them for their faithful involvement in the group building process. Mention that this is the last week in the month-long focus on group building but that you hope the group will always work at being more of a team together.

Explain this final step in the process of building community, then begin with Week in Review (page 143). Say: "We're going to do a little exercise called Week in Review that I think will help us get a big handle on our week and a smaller handle on our future." Give the group members the directions and encourage them to proceed.

When they've finished, say: "Now that we've examined our week, let's continue to examine our lives. Let's work together on a little strategy called Overcoming Adversity." See page 135 for the directions to this exercise.

When that exercise is over, thank the youth for their openness. Say, "Let's conclude our four-week focus by doing an affirming activity." If your group is 20 or less, do Gifts (page 86). If larger than that, do another Group Hug (page 87). People never get enough of those.

Conclude with a pizza or banana split party—or both if you dare!

ONE-DAY FORMAT

Now let's look at another way to build community in your group—the one-day format. This format is especially good early in the school year or at some other time when many newcomers have become involved with the group and a feeling of community doesn't seem to exist any longer. It's a one-day crash course in group building. In the 12 hours you are together as a group, you will move through all five steps in the process of building community.

Prior to the one-day event, stress that all participants need to be on time to really enjoy the experience. Following is the schedule for the one-day event.

EVENT SCHEDULE

9:00 a.m.   **Introduction.** Welcome the group members. Tell them how much fun you expect to have and why; for example, getting to know new people, eating some great food, playing some new games, thinking about life.

Explain the process of building community and focus on the first step: bond building. Say that bond building is where we begin to become more of a "team" by getting to know one another better, sharing common experiences and having fun. Then say, "We're going to begin with a game called Blind Alphabet." See page 32 for instructions. Move quickly through the discussion questions since it's still early in the day (the activities are best when the atmosphere is lively).

Move on to another bond building exercise called Climbing the Walls. Say, "Now that you've proved yourself blindfolded, let's try something a little more difficult." Introduce Climbing the Walls (page 36). If you have 12 or more participants, divide into two teams. When you've completed the exercise, have the group members sit in a circle and answer the discussion questions.

Play another bond building activity called Nuclear Holocaust. Introduce this activity by saying, "You've proven to yourself that you can use your bodies in Climbing the Walls, now let's do a little test of your minds." Give the directions for Nuclear Holocaust (page 46).

After you've completed these three bond building exercises, debrief the group by asking these questions:

1. What do these exercises have to do with group building?

2. How do you think you as a group have become more of a unit?

3. What did you learn from these first three activities?

After the discussion, tell the youth, "We're going

to continue building these bonds as a group by participating in an exercise called Trust Fall.'' Give them directions (page 53). When you come to the discussion time, use the discussion questions only. It's still too early in the day for the teachable moment questions.

Your group members are now ready to move to the first opening up exercise Questions (page 67). Introduce this next step by saying: ''In the preceding exercises, we began to become more of a community—more of a team. We know each other better; we've had some common experiences; we've shared in some fun; we know we can trust each other. The second step in building community is called opening up. We've got a series of non-threatening questions we'd like you to look at as a group.'' Introduce the opening up exercise Questions and give the directions.

10:30 a.m. **Break.** Take a short break, then move to the Faith Collage, the second in the opening up exercises. Introduce the activity by saying: ''In Questions, we looked at many aspects in our lives. Now I'd like us to focus on a more specific subject—our faith— through an exercise called Faith Collage.'' Give the youth the directions (page 60).

11:30 a.m. **Affirming.** Two steps have been completed: bond building and opening up. Now you and the group are ready to move to step three—affirming. Explain the concept of affirming to the group members and ask them to do the exercise Gift Certificates (page 86). If your group is larger than 20, divide into several groups to play Gift Certificates. Regather as a total group and ask the general questions:

1. What did you appreciate most about this activity?

2. What did you learn?

Noon **Lunch.** Lead the students through the bond building exercise called Servant's Lunch, but don't tell the participants how it will be done in advance. When the group members have gathered, ask the blessing on the food and then tell them about Servant's Lunch (page 51). Go through the discussion questions at the conclusion of the lunch.

12:45 p.m. **Break.** Servant's Lunch is not a break since the youth have been tied to one another. A break time is

	important to give the students a bit of "breathing space" and refreshment.
1:00 p.m.	**Games.** Play some games—the wilder, the better. For some good game ideas, take a look at **Fun 'n Games** by Rice, Rydberg and Yaconelli published by Zondervan. Another excellent game resource is the **Try This One** series published by Group Books.
1:30 p.m.	**Stretching.** After the games, call the group together and introduce the stretching phase of the program: Hard Bargain. This exercise can lead to great frustration and great teaching, but it will stretch the group. You will need four hours for this event. Don't let the students know about this event in advance; advance notice will diminish the learning experience. Only you and a couple other trusted confidants—all sworn to absolute secrecy—should know.

In advance, read over the instructions for Hard Bargain (page 99). Run the meeting according to those instructions and make sure you give enough time for debriefing through the discussion questions. The schedule for Hard Bargain should look like this:

1:30 p.m.	UNO.
2:00 p.m.	Swim.
5:00 p.m.	Movie.
5:30 p.m.	Dinner.
6:00 p.m.	**Discussion.** Debrief Hard Bargain.
6:30 p.m.	**Review.** Discuss where the group members have been today. "For almost 10 hours we've been together focusing on the subject of group building. We have moved through four steps: bond building when we played Blind Alphabet, Climbing the Walls, Nuclear Holocaust, Trust Fall and Servant's Lunch; opening up when we played Questions and Faith Collage; affirming with the Gift Certificates; stretching with our last activity Hard Bargain.

"In the next two hours, we're going to move into the last step: deeper sharing and goal setting. We will participate in two deeper sharing exercises called I Need and The Wall. After each one of these, we will do an affirming exercise." Give the directions for I Need (page 133).

7:30 p.m.	**Affirming.** Introduce Candle With Care (page 82).
7:50 p.m.	**Deeper Sharing.** Introduce The Wall (page 142).
8:30 p.m.	**Closing.** Conclude with a Group Hug (page 87). Share what the day has meant to you and allow

others to share what the day has meant to them.
Close in prayer.

CHAPTER 8:
RETREATS

The previous chapter gave you two meeting formats for introducing group building to your young people. This chapter will give you ideas for bringing your group together in a way not possible in a simple week night meeting or an all-day event.

Listed in this chapter are four retreat and camp ideas which emphasize the five-step group building process. The camps and retreats vary in length—from three to seven days. They vary in location—from the city to a winter snow lodge or a summer resident camp. These ready-made, easy-to-use group building ideas are ideal for creating group unity and fellowship in a relatively short period of time.

This chapter isn't the authoritative word on camping and retreats as such. For that we recommend another book by our publisher, **The Group Retreat Book** by Arlo Reichter and others. That book is a complete retreat planning guide which contains 34 retreat designs for junior and senior high youth groups. It's a winner—almost everything you'll ever want to know about retreats.

This chapter is primarily written to inspire you to use more of these group building exercises in your retreat and camping experiences. Two of the examples in this chapter are universal. Everyone can do a Week-Long Residence Camp somewhere nearby whether it be in a retreat center, camp or church. And everyone can do an Urban Retreat in his or her town or a larger neighboring city. But two of the retreat examples are not-so-universal. The Snow Retreat does require snow, but because it's a cross-country snow retreat, it doesn't require mountains. That's a break for people who live in the flatlands. But one of the amazing things I learned traveling around the country doing seminars for youth workers is that in every state, groups do snow camps. Some groups just have to travel farther to do them. The premise is simple: If you have snow, use it. If you don't have snow, go to it. The second not-so-universal idea is a Rock Climbing and Rafting Retreat. If you don't have rocks or rivers, you can't use the retreat as it is specifically described in this chapter. What you *can* do is substitute. Look at the stretching exercises in Chapter 5. And ask yourself: What do people do for adventure in our "neck of the woods"? How can I incorporate those adventures into a retreat where community will be built? Simply use these ideas as a springboard for your own.

WEEK-LONG RESIDENCE CAMP

Group building can tremendously enhance a traditional summer camp. A speaker's message is far more effective when delivered among campers who trust one another. By making a camp "small group oriented," lasting personal growth is far more likely to occur.

The Week-Long Residence Camp is small group oriented and it takes all the participants through the five steps of building community. Below are a few tips and comments about this type of camp, followed by a detailed schedule of activities.

Quality Counselors

In a small-group-oriented camp, high-quality counselors are of great importance. Select mature counselors who have a desire to serve. They must be willing to forego the late-night staff parties typical of some camps. Counselors must be at camp for one reason only: to bring campers closer to God.

Cooks, recreation leaders, speakers, lifeguards and directors should *not* be counselors. Counseling is more than a full-time job. A counselor's job is to be *with* the kids—24 hours a day.

Core Groups

Each counselor is placed in a cabin with four or five youth from his or her church. The counselors are asked to get to know the kids during the week and stay in touch with them afterward. The camp's effectiveness is greatly enhanced when counselors follow up with the participants once the week is over.

For this camp, most group building occurs in "core groups" (one guys' cabin combined with one girls' cabin totalling eight to 10 students and two counselors). These core groups participate together in each of the camp's activities and attend the same seminars, allowing for follow-up discussion. The core groups also are placed on the same teams during all-camp games, allowing shy and "loner" students to participate with friends they've learned to trust.

Rules and Regulations

In this type of a camp, very little needs to be announced about rules and regulations. Each counselor polices his or her own campers. Each counselor is responsible for making sure his or her campers attend required meetings, come in at night and behave in proper manner. Since counselors are spending every waking moment with their four or five campers, discipline problems are less frequent.

One-on-One

Instruct the counselors to meet one-on-one with each of their campers for 20 to 30 minutes of discussion sometime late in the week. Afternoon "free time" easily can be utilized for this. Free time also can be used to befriend loners and get to know other kids.

One-on-one time frequently proves to be the highlight of the week for the counselors, as they are given opportunities to talk with each camper about the status of his or her personal relationship with Jesus Christ.

CAMP SCHEDULE

Day One

3:00 p.m. **Registration.**

4:00 p.m. **Core Groups.** Place each core group in a room or cabin out of sight and sound from other groups. Start with introductions. Have one student tell his name and an animal which he feels characterizes him (John-tiger). The second person repeats the identity and animal of the first person then shares about herself (John-tiger, Susan-butterfly). This process is repeated (John-tiger, Susan-butterfly, Sally-hummingbird, Bill-aardvark, Pete-orangutan) until the entire group has been introduced.

Explain to the core group members that they will be doing a number of wild and out-of-the-ordinary events as a group during the week. Without any further introduction, have the group participate in three bond building exercises: Knots (page 41), Points of Contact (page 47), Trust Fall (page 53).

After completing the bond building exercises, sit the group members down and have them answer:

1. What were the purposes of each of these

exercises?

2. What did you learn about yourself through them?

Next, describe Three Minutes (page 71). Instruct the group to listen as each person shares about himself or herself. Remember, a counselor should go first, modeling a high level of vulnerable sharing.

5:30 p.m. **Supper.**

6:15 p.m. **All-Camp Bond Building Exercises.** Stand Up (page 52), Lap Sit (page 42), Electric Fence (page 37).

No debriefing is necessary for these exercises. Since the emphasis is on having fun and getting acquainted.

6:30 p.m. **Break.**

7:00 p.m. **Wild All-Camp Games.** Wild camp games effectively draw youth together through shared fun. Rowdy events allow teenagers to unleash energy and keep them attentive during meetings and core group sessions.

Select games from **Fun 'n Games** by Rice, Rydberg and Yaconelli published by Zondervan, or the **Try This One** series published by Group Books.

Select teams by combining several core groups for each side. This will ensure that even the "loner" kids will know a few people on their team.

For this group building retreat, don't overemphasize competition. Competitive activities can be fun and profitable, but you shouldn't keep week-long tabs on winners and losers. Instead, talk about the teamwork and cooperation necessary to function effectively as a group. Reorganize teams from event to event, pairing different core groups together.

8:30 p.m. **Evening Service.** These 90-minute evening sessions will provide campers with the "meat and potatoes" of the week. The speakers will only need to stimulate discussion, because the core groups will meet immediately following each service to talk about personal application of each speaker's message.

In the evening services, utilize singing as a means to prepare campers' hearts and minds for the message. Start with rowdy songs and move to more mellow, worshipful choruses. An attentive tone will thus be set for the speakers.

Following each service, send campers immediately

	to their core groups for discussion.
10:00 p.m.	**Core Groups.** This session continues with the opening up process. Don't use this hour to have an indepth discussion about the evening service. That will come later in the week after the students know and trust each other better.

Introduce the opening up exercise Questions (page 67). Allow the youth to select their own vulnerability level. Ask clarifying questions, but not probing ones.

Make sure the students remain attentive when it is another's turn to speak. The atmosphere set at these first core groups will determine the degree of their success.

At this point, counselors should tell the campers that they will spend one-on-one discussion time with each of them at some point during the week. These one-on-one times will be of extreme benefit to the counselor. The campers will be asked how they currently view their Christian life and what goals they are setting for after the camp.

11:30 p.m.	**Lights Out.**

Day Two

6:30 a.m.	**Counselor Meeting.** Counselor meetings hold a camp together. Allowing counselors to pray together, share frustrations, talk through the day's schedule and center upon God's presence are key to the lives of 24-hour-a-day counselors. Here is a suggested counselor meeting format:
6:30 a.m.	Counselors arrive, maintaining a "discipline of silence" as they enter, focusing on God and his presence.
6:40 a.m.	Sing three worship songs and pray.
6:45 a.m.	Ask counselors to share their feelings about the week thus far. What victories and struggles have they had? (Encourage them to share experiences without actually using specific campers' names.)
7:00 a.m.	Allow each of the major program staff (main speaker, seminar leaders, recreation coordinator, etc.) to share his or her plans for the day's activities. This is important. Communication between staff and counselors assists both parties' effectiveness. For example, "Counselors, could you help me by 'policing' the campers in the back row?" Or,

"Speaker, I think my campers need to hear a message on 'discipline.' "

7:15 a.m.   Break into groups of threes or fours, share prayer requests and pray. These groups should remain intact throughout the week, allowing counselors to lift up one another in prayer.

7:30 a.m.   As each small group of counselors concludes prayer, have them quietly exit and return to their cabins to awaken their campers.

8:00 a.m.   **Breakfast.**

9:00 a.m.   **Personal Devotions.** Instruct the counselors to select Bible passages for their campers to read for devotions. Allow campers to go off on their own for 15 to 20 minutes to read the assigned passage and pray. Reunite in cabin groups and let each camper share what God taught him or her through his or her time alone. Another option is to have the main speaker assign the Bible passages.

9:30 a.m.   **Core Groups.** Begin this session with an active bond builder such as Nuclear Holocaust (page 46). Remember, one leader should participate in each exercise while the other "spots." Debrief the game, using the accompanying discussion questions.

Now have the students stand and participate in an opening up exercise called Forced Choice (page 62). Discuss why people chose as they did.

Conclude this gathering by having each camper spend a few minutes creating an imaginary life in Fantasy Island (page 61).

10:30 a.m.   **Seminars.** Select several topics of specific interest to students for camp seminars. "How to Get Along With Your Parents," "How to Keep Faith and Keep Friends," "Love, Sex and Dating," "How I Can Tell My Friends About Jesus," and "Talking With God" are all possible subjects and titles.

Allow cabin groups to choose seminars to attend together. By keeping cabin groups intact, follow-up discussion regarding a seminar becomes simple and easy.

Noon   **Servant's Lunch.** See page 51 for directions.

1:00 p.m.   **Core Groups.** Divide your group into smaller groups of three to four each. Assign an adult leader or a mature student to each group. Pass out Triad Booklets (page 71) and have the youth take turns answering the questions.

The stage has now been set for the third step in building community: affirming. Candle With Care (page 82) is a great exercise for group members who may not know one another real well. As a leader, you should select students to affirm who may not get affirmed otherwise. Close with prayer and a Group Hug (page 87).

2:30 p.m.	**Wild All-Camp Games.**
3:30 p.m.	**Free Time.**
5:30 p.m.	**Supper.**
6:30 p.m.	**Bus Cram.** See if you can fit the entire group into a bus or a van (as many as 40 can fit in a van). Be careful to load and unload quickly in order to avoid claustrophobia.
7:00 p.m.	**Evening Service.**
8:30 p.m.	**Core Groups.** Campers are now ready for some personal application of the speaker's message.

Begin this session with an opening up exercise called Symbols (page 70). Have each camper spend about 10 minutes alone outside, finding a symbol from nature which he or she feels represents his or her current relationship with God. Reunite the group and have each person share his or her symbol and its meaning with the rest of the core group.

Spend the rest of this session discussing the speaker's talk. Begin by having the group restate the central theme of the evening's message. Then ask the following questions:

1. What statements of the speaker impacted you the most?

2. How can you relate these thoughts to your own personal life?

If possible, obtain questions prepared in advance by the speaker for these follow-up discussions. Utilize these questions and some of your own to maximize the effectiveness of each talk.

9:30 p.m.	**Wild All-Camp Games.**
11:30 p.m.	**Lights Out.**

Day Three

6:30 a.m.	**Counselor Meeting.**
8:00 a.m.	**Breakfast.**
9:00 a.m.	**Personal Devotions.**
9:30 a.m.	**Core Groups.** This is another affirming session.

First, however, begin with a simple bond building exercise such as Line Up on a Log (page 43). Be sure to "spot" this exercise to avoid twisted ankles.

Warm Fuzzies (page 90) is an in-depth, extremely productive and fun affirming activity. As each person is placed on the "hot seat" for several minutes of compliments, the group draws together.

11:00 a.m.	**Core Groups.** The core groups now need to be "tested" in their caring for one another through stretching experiences. Placed together in somewhat difficult and uncomfortable settings, campers learn to rely on one another for emotional support.

Community Service (page 95) brings the group closer together as well as gives campers an opportunity for showing compassion and servanthood for needy people.

Locate a residential community (for some camps this will require some traveling) in which members of the core groups can divide into pairs and go door-to-door asking to do work projects for people free of charge.

Work for several hours. Tell campers that they may *not* ask for food for lunch. If they are offered food, they may eat it. Otherwise, they fast. This gives them an empathy for the needy and a reliance upon God for their provisions.

Return to camp at about 3:00 and spend 30 minutes debriefing this activity in core groups using the discussion questions accompanying this exercise (page 96).

3:30 p.m.	**Free Time.**
5:30 p.m.	**Supper.**
6:15 p.m.	**Skit Night Preparation.** All core groups are asked to prepare an act for the upcoming evening of skits.
7:00 p.m.	**Wild All-Camp Games.**
8:30 p.m.	**Evening Service.**
10:00 p.m.	**Core Groups.** Form a circle. Discuss the speaker's message and its relevance to the persons in the core group. Go around the circle and allow each camper to share the talk's personal application to him or her.
11:30 p.m.	**Lights Out.**

Day Four

6:30 a.m.	**Counselor Meeting.**

8:00 a.m.	**Breakfast.**
9:00 a.m.	**Personal Devotions.**
9:30 a.m.	**Core Groups.** Finally, your group has reached the deeper sharing level! To each member, pass out the cartoon from All Aboard (page 124). Allow each member to share which figure in the drawing best represents how he or she feels in this core group. See the discussion questions provided with this exercise. This activity can be an enlightening time for your group.
10:30 a.m.	**Seminars.**
Noon	**Lunch.**
1:00 p.m.	**Stretching.** Select stretching experiences or develop your own depending upon your camp's access to these activities. For example, Ropes Course, Rock Climbing, Hard Bargain, etc.
5:30 p.m.	**Supper.**
6:15 p.m.	**Skit Night Preparation.**
7:00 p.m.	**Evening Service.**
8:30 p.m.	**Core Groups.** Again utilize this session to talk about the speaker's message.
9:30 p.m.	**Wild All-Camp Games.**
11:30 p.m.	**Lights Out.**

Day Five

6:30 a.m.	**Counselor Meeting.**
8:00 a.m.	**Breakfast.**
9:00 a.m.	**Personal Devotions.**
9:30 a.m.	**Core Groups.** Instruct each camper to spend several minutes alone, contemplating the current status of his or her commitment to God. Utilize the deeper sharing activity The Wall (page 142) as a means to stimulate the participants' thoughts. Gather and share "walls" with one another.
10:30 a.m.	**Seminars.**
Noon	**Lunch.**
1:00 p.m.	**Seminars.**
2:30 p.m.	**Free Time.**
4:30 p.m.	**Wild All-Camp Games.**
5:30 p.m.	**Supper.**
6:15 p.m.	**Skit Night Preparation.**
7:00 p.m.	**Skit Night.** This traditional camp activity continues to be successful year after year. Campers never cease to enjoy performing on stage. Years after a camp is over, a camper still can remember the skit in which

he or she acted. By performing skits according to core groups, this opportunity to be on stage is also an opportunity for a bond building exercise—selecting a skit, fine-tuning the details and finally performing it.

Counselors beware! Don't succumb to the temptation to be the ringleader of your core group's skit. Allow the campers to talk through this dilemma, proving their own capabilities.

9:00 p.m.	**Evening Service.**
10:30 p.m.	**Core Groups.** Rehash the speaker's message and its implications for each person.
11:30 p.m.	**Lights Out.**

Day Six

6:30 a.m.	**Counselor Meeting.**
8:00 a.m.	**Breakfast.**
9:00 a.m.	**Personal Devotions.**
9:30 a.m.	**Core Groups.** Ask the campers to think back over the previous year and its victories and struggles. Lead them in the opening up exercise Year in Review (page 76).
10:30 a.m.	**Seminars.**
Noon	**Lunch.**
1:00 p.m.	**Wild All-Camp Games.**
2:00 p.m.	**Free Time.**
4:30 p.m.	**Core Groups.** As the camp nears its completion, a discussion must center on the topic: Where do we go from here? Obviously, a camp setting is a "make believe" setting. It is not real life. Therefore, campers need to become aware that life "back home" will not remain on this group "high"; that the group will naturally return to real life soon after the camp ends. However, some of the impact of the camp will remain with them forever. Share with them this "Slinky Theory":

"Slinkies" (those wiry toys that expand and contract like an accordian, and which most young kids own sometime in life) seldom remain in their original shape. Soon after purchase, kids stretch them out so far, that when they let go of Slinkies, they don't contract to their previous shape. They grow a few inches.

This camp has been an attempt to "stretch your

'Slinky.' '' When you return home, you won't be able to remain fully outstretched. However, once the "dust has settled," you will have "grown a few inches" from where you were before this camp.

The cohesive bond which you now feel with the members of this group; the closeness you feel with God—these feelings will fade somewhat with time. However, your relationship with God and with the people in this group *have* grown this week. And this fact will remain even after the warm feelings have faded.

Continue this discussion by utilizing the deeper sharing exercise called I Need (page 133). Relate this activity to the future of this small group. Close by having students answer this question: "What have I learned through this core group which I can take home with me?"

5:30 p.m.	**Supper.**
6:30 p.m.	**Free Time.**
7:00 p.m.	**Wild All-Camp Games.**
9:00 p.m.	**Evening Service.**
10:30 p.m.	**Core Groups.** Apply the speaker's message to your own lives. Have the campers do the deeper sharing exercise The Ideal Life (page 132).
11:30 p.m.	**Lights Out.**

Day Seven

6:30 a.m.	**Counselor Meeting.**
8:00 a.m.	**Breakfast.**
9:00 a.m.	**Personal Devotions.**
9:30 a.m.	**Core Groups.** For this last core group session, do two affirming exercises: Gifts (page 86) and Group Hug (page 87).
10:30 a.m.	**Pack Up/Clean Up.**
11:30 a.m.	**Goodbyes.** All-camp Group Hug (page 87).

SNOW RETREAT

The Snow Retreat is usually a winter event unless you live in Siberia. The retreat is unique in that the primary activity—cross-country skiing—becomes a stretching experience itself. The stretching of skiing is combined with the other steps in the process of building community.

Below are a few tips and comments about this type of a retreat, followed by a detailed schedule of activities.

Activities

When you plan the retreat, make the main activity cross-country skiing. Many youth groups have downhill-skiing retreats; however, these are not conducive to group development. Downhill skiing is an individualistic activity where most time is spent with just one or two other people.

Another winter retreat option that many church groups choose is tubing. Again, this has its drawbacks. Tubing is probably the most dangerous activity in which youth groups take part. More accidents occur from tubing than any of the other activities suggested here. Some insurance companies will not even cover tubing any longer because it is such a high-risk activity. For that reason, we can't recommend it.

Cross-country skiing is fairly easy and fun to learn. Ask a sponsor who knows how to cross-country ski to spend 30 minutes in instruction with your youth group. Or see if the ski shop has an instructor who can spend time with your group. Most ski resorts offer cross-country ski lessons. Also, most ski resorts rent cross-country skis. Reserve them for your group to guarantee that you will have enough at the time of your retreat.

Staff

Since this retreat is going to be a time of group development, it is important to have all your regular youth group leaders there to facilitate quality follow-up.

Facilities

An inexpensive location for this retreat is a church which has a multi-purpose room and kitchen and is located near a ski area. If that is not possible, then locate a chalet or cabin which is near a ski resort.

SNOW RETREAT SCHEDULE

Day One

7:30 p.m.   **Arrival.** As soon as everyone has arrived at the retreat facility and is out of the cars, *don't* unload the baggage. Start the retreat by encouraging the participants to make as much as possible of the opportunity. Remind them that it is their retreat. You are there to facilitate the activities, but their attitude will determine the outcome.

Play a variation of Bouncing Ball Discussion from **Try This One ... Strikes Again** published by Group Books. One person holds a ball and begins by saying his or her name and what he or she expects from this retreat; for example, "My name is Lee. I hope to get to know everybody better." Lee bounces the ball to another person who continues: "My name is Jeff. I hope I learn how to cross-country ski." Continue until everyone has had a chance to participate. Do the Bouncing Ball Discussion and, as the leader, enjoy it. Convey the idea that you are having a good time.

8:00 p.m.   **Snack Time.** Have a snack and then give everyone 15 minutes to unload the vehicles and take their gear to their sleeping quarters.

8:30 p.m.   **Bond Building.** Do several bond building exercises to get the group comfortable with each other. Use the following: Nuclear Holocaust (page 46), Blind Alphabet (page 33), Line Up on a Log (page 43).

Don't use the discussion questions at the end of each exercise. Debrief the students by asking:

1. What was the most difficult part of these exercises for you?

2. What did you learn from these exercises?

9:00 p.m.   **Opening Up.** Then do Questions (page 67).

Discuss tomorrow's activities. Tell the youth the time for breakfast and what everyone should wear for skiing. Have everyone share one goal and one fear about the retreat.

9:30 p.m.   **Games.** Play a couple of rowdy games to get the participants worn out before bedtime. **Fun 'n Games** by Rice, Rydberg and Yaconelli is a good resource. Also use the **Try This One** series published by Group Books.

10:30 p.m.   **Bedtime.**

Day Two

6:30 a.m.   **Staff Meeting.** This is an important time to get the staff prepared for the retreat activities. Talk through each day's schedule and answer any questions from the staff. Encourage your staff to have a positive attitude, no matter what happens, throughout the day.

7:00 a.m.   **Rise and Shine.**

7:30 a.m.   **Breakfast.** Eat a hot breakfast before going cross-country skiing.

8:00 a.m.   **Devotions.** For a morning devotional do Symbols and have each person find an object that represents his or her current relationship with God (page 70).

Then, to get everyone feeling good about each other, do Names in a Hat (page 88).

8:45 a.m.   **Skiing.** Leave for skiing. See Cross-Country Skiing (page 96).

Noon   **Lunch.**

3:15 p.m.   **Arrival.** Go back to the retreat facility. Give everyone a chance to change clothes and warm up.

3:45 p.m.   **Hard Bargain.** It is important that everyone is feeling good about each other before Hard Bargain, so take time to do the affirming exercise Celebration (page 82). Ask the youth to share specifically about the time during the retreat.

Hard Bargain is a stretching exercise that can lead to great frustration as well as great teaching. You will need four hours for this event. Don't let the students know about this event in advance. Advance notice will diminish the learning experience. Only you and a couple other trusted confidants—all sworn to absolute secrecy—should know.

In advance, read over the instructions for Hard Bargain (page 99). Run the meeting according to those instructions and make sure you give enough time for debriefing through the discussion questions. The Hard Bargain schedule should look like this:

4:00 p.m.   UNO.

4:30 p.m.   Hand out money and leave for a swimming pool.

4:45 p.m.   Swimming.

6:00 p.m.   Arrive back at retreat facility. Prepare and eat dinner.

7:00 p.m.   Movie.

7:30 p.m.   Snack.

7:45 p.m.   Debrief Hard Bargain.

8:15 p.m.   **Affirming.** Spend some time doing Affirmation Collage (page 81).

9:00 p.m.   **Games.** Play a couple of rowdy games to get the youth worn out before bedtime.

10:00 p.m.   **Bedtime.**

Day Three

8:00 a.m.   **Staff Meeting.** Discuss how your leaders feel the activities are going. Talk about any participants who have needs for some additional attention. Close with a time of prayer for the day's activities.

8:30 a.m.	**Breakfast.**
9:30 a.m.	**Worship.** Have a worship service that includes a time of singing and praying. Do a deeper sharing exercise called The Ideal Life (page 132).
11:30 a.m.	**Closing.** As a closing, do the affirming exercise Telegrams (page 89) and another affirming exercise Group Hug (page 87).
Noon	**Departure.** Load vehicles and leave.

URBAN RETREAT

This retreat idea is designed for use in the city. As a means to build community, the group members will work on service projects, visit an inner-city mission and witness to strangers. Following is a detailed schedule:

URBAN RETREAT SCHEDULE

Day One

6:30 p.m.   **Arrival.** Take the participants to a church or retreat facility located in a metropolitan area.

7:00 p.m.   **Friday Evening Session.** This session is designed to help students get better acquainted before the busy weekend begins. Bond building, opening up and affirming exercises are used to bring this about.

Begin by introducing the retreat to the students. Explain that their "comfort zones" will most definitely be stretched during the next 24 hours. They will have some unique opportunities to serve hurting people and strengthen their relationships with members of the group. Instill in them a degree of both anticipation and trepidation about the events which await them.

Do three bond building games to begin the evening's activities: Radioactive Swamp (page 48), Climbing the Walls (page 36), Trust Walk (page 54).

Debrief these exercises when all three are completed. Do not use the discussion questions at the end of each exercise; use the following:

1. What purpose do you see in these exercises?
2. What did you learn?

Move into the opening up stage by allowing each participant to share for Three Minutes (page 71) about his or her life. As a leader, you go first, modeling a deeper level of vulnerability. If three minutes seem too long a time to talk for most of the group, cut it to two minutes each.

Conclude this session with an affirming exercise called Ten (page 89).

9:15 p.m.   **Games.** Play some rowdy games to wear out the youth before bedtime. Consult **Fun 'n Games** by Rice, Rydberg and Yaconelli or the **Try This One** series published by Group Books.

10:15 p.m.   **Snacks.**

10:45 p.m.   **Lights Out.**

Day Two

6:45 a.m.   **Wake Up.**

7:30 a.m.   **Big Breakfast.**

8:30 a.m.   **Saturday Morning Session.** Open this session with another bond building game Nuclear Holocaust (page 46). Move to a deeper sharing level by using the teachable moment questions in the designated box to debrief this game.

Encourage each student to share with the group his or her fears regarding the activities of the day with the question, "What portion of this retreat are you most fearful?" Share your fears as well. Then pray together as a group.

Conclude with the affirming exercise Names in a Hat (page 88).

10:00 a.m.   **Community Service.** Divide the students into small groups of fours or fives. Send them door-to-door and have them ask if there are work projects they can do free of charge (see Community Service, page 95). Or, work with a community action program in the neighborhood that can connect your group with needy people.

Instruct the students that they may not ask for food for lunch. If they are offered food, they may eat it; if not, they fast. This will give the students empathy for the needy and dependence upon God for their provisions. Make sure to tell the students *not* to accept money or gifts from the residents. Tell the students to respond to offers of money or gifts with, "Thank you for your offer but we are doing this as a gift of love. Being here with you is our reward. Thank you very much."

Meet back at the "home base" at 3:00 p.m. to debrief this activity. See the questions for discussion on page 96.

3:00 p.m.   **Discussion.** Debrief the Community Service.

5:30 p.m.   **Mission.** Travel to an inner-city mission, serve dinner, spend the night, and serve breakfast and lunch. See Night at a Mission (page 107). You must prepare well in advance with the mission staff.

9:00 p.m.   **Sharing Your Faith.** Instruct the students to join in pairs and tell some strangers about their personal relationship with Jesus Christ. See Sharing Your Faith (page 115). Many metropolitan areas have downtown Christian coffeehouses made specifically for this purpose. Check them out. If not, have the youth share with men and women at the mission.

Day Three

6:30 a.m.	**Wake Up.**
9:30 a.m.	**Worship.** Attend the mission worship service.
2:00 p.m.	**Return.** Leave the mission and go back to the church or retreat facility. Debrief Night at a Mission and Sharing Your Faith by using the discussion questions on page 116.
3:00 p.m.	**Sunday Afternoon Session.** Wrap up the weekend with the deeper sharing exercise Over the Hill (page 136). Encourage each student to discuss the following questions:

    1. What stands out most in your mind about this weekend?

    2. What did you learn about service to others through this weekend?

    3. In what ways did you grow closer to the members of this group?

    4. How do you want this weekend to affect your life in the future?

4:15 p.m.	**Group Hug.** The Group Hug (page 87), the sharing and the warm goodbyes will cap this wonderful weekend.

ROCK CLIMBING AND RAFTING RETREAT

For this retreat, you will need a rock and some water. If you don't have them, go where they are or make some substitutions.

This 48-hour extravaganza of rock climbing and whitewater rafting has proven to be an extremely successful format for building community. This is a very popular program because of the unique mixture of activities, short duration of time and low cost. The stretching, trust-developing experience in rock climbing combined with the exhilaration and teamwork of whitewater rafting accomplishes a great deal in the lives of participants. The activities throughout the trip are designed to stimulate discussion about group unity, trust, self-worth and faith in God.

Below are a few comments and guidelines followed by a detailed schedule.

Outfitter

The quality of the outfitter will determine the quality of the retreat. Some questions to ask the outfitters to determine whether or not you can work effectively with them are:

1. What qualifications do you look for when hiring staff?
2. What does staff training consist of?
3. How long have you been running wilderness trips?
4. How many years of experience does the average staff person have?
5. What first-aid background does your staff have?
6. What is your philosophy of ministry?
7. What is your camper-staff ratio?
8. What are the camping facilities like?
9. What insurance do you provide your customers?

If you have problems locating an outfitter, contact the authors of this resource at Group Books, Box 481, Loveland, Colorado. They will send you the address of a qualified outfitter near you.

Let the outfitter know you are more interested in developing group unity rather than personal character growth. Let the outfitter know that group successes and teachable moments should be highlighted rather than individual ones. Some wilderness agencies put a high value on stretching participants to their breaking point. In a short 48-hour activity, this should not be your goal.

After you have contracted with the outfitter, give him or her as much information about your group members and their special needs as possible (how they interact as a group, the group's expectations, anyone who will need special attention, etc.).

Based on the experience of the outfitter, you will need to decide who is running the bulk of the programming. In what areas do each of you have the last word?

We do not suggest that you should undertake providing the equipment and technical staff yourself. Even if you have access to some skilled rock climbers and rafters, they need to have experience teaching and leading novices. Otherwise, they will have no idea what to expect. Getting all the equipment together on your own also can be very time consuming, costly, and can result in using equipment that does not meet proper safety standards.

Staff

Since this retreat is going to be a time of group development, it is important to have all the regular group leaders there, even though they may be more afraid of the activities than the students.

Parents

Parents will naturally be concerned with the safety of the retreat. For this reason it is wise to precede the event with a parents' night. Have the outfitter give a slide show and demonstrate all safety measures. Participants will not need to be in prime physical shape to enjoy the program. Rock climbing varies in its degree of difficulty, allowing each person to climb areas which will challenge him or her.

Pre-Trip Promotion

How you promote the trip to the potential participants will determine their mind-set going into the trip and will determine the outcome of the retreat. With this in mind, take serious thought on how you publicize the trip. Let the participants know about the sleeping arrangements; the quality of food (whether it is being cooked on Coleman stoves or gourmet food from a camp kitchen); showers or the lack of them; the goals of your trip.

If the kids think they are just signing up for a fun time and then you get serious on them, you will find them unwilling to participate. Let them know that there will be a time to debrief the different activities. Don't, however, give them a copy of the whole schedule.

Let them know that it is a very action-packed retreat with a fairly tight schedule.

Necessary Supplies

Tell each person to bring: wool socks or wet-suit booties, a T-shirt, two pairs of tennis shoes, a hat, rain gear, a sleeping bag, a towel, a complete change of clothes for after rafting, sunglasses, a modest swimsuit, a wool sweater, suntan lotion, modest shorts, a flashlight, baggy pants (for rock climbing). You also will need to ask each participant to fill out a medical release. Tell the youth to leave their tape decks and radios at home.

RETREAT SCHEDULE

Day One

7:30 p.m.   **Arrival.** Group arrives at base camp. As soon as everyone is out of the cars, *don't* unload the baggage. Start the retreat off by encouraging participants to make as much as possible of the opportunity. Remind them that it is their retreat. You are there to facilitate the activities, but their attitude will determine the outcome.

Play the game Don't Get Burned from **Try This One ... Too** published by Group Books. Using a book of matches, each person one-at-a-time reveals as many things about who he or she is before the match burns out.

8:00 p.m.	**Snack Time.** Have a snack and then give everyone 15 minutes to unload the vehicles and take their stuff to their sleeping quarters.
8:15 p.m.	**Bond Building.** Do several bond building exercises to get the group comfortable with each other: Knots (page 41), Electric Fence (page 37), Trust Fall (page 53). Debrief these exercises by asking the following questions:

    1. What do you see as the purpose in doing these exercises?

    2. What did it feel like to fall back in the group's arms?

    3. What did you learn from doing these?

9:00 p.m.	**Opening Up.** Continue with Three Minutes (page 71). This is a crucial time for setting the tone of the the retreat. Begin with the leader and have him or her model a serious, vulnerable attitude. Let the students take longer than three minutes to talk about themselves if they need them.
9:45 p.m.	**Discussion.** Talk about tomorrow's activities. Go over the schedule for wake up and breakfast and say what everyone should wear for rock climbing. Have everyone share one goal and one fear about rock climbing.
10:30 p.m.	**Bedtime.**

Day Two

6:30 a.m.	**Staff Meeting.** This is an important time to get the staff prepared for the upcoming activities. Make sure that your rock climbing guides are present. Talk through the schedule and answer any questions from the staff. Encourage your staff to have a positive attitude, no matter what happens, throughout the day.
7:00 a.m.	**Rise and Shine.**
7:30 a.m.	**Breakfast.**
8:00 a.m.	**Quiet Time.** Have everyone go off alone to read 1 Corinthians 12:12-26. Have the youth think through which body part best describes them and why. Get the group members back together after 15 minutes to share their response. Then do an affirming exercise called Names in a Hat (page 88).
9:00 a.m.	**Rock Climbing.** Pack up and leave for rock climbing. Be sure to take plenty of water to drink. See Rock Climbing (page 112).

12:30 p.m.	**Lunch.** Take a break for Servant's Lunch (page 51). After lunch do some more rock climbing.
4:30 p.m.	**Swimming.** Climb until everyone has had an opportunity to do as much as they want. Then clean off those sweaty bodies by going swimming. If the area does not have a lifeguard, make sure someone in the group is a qualified lifeguard.
6:00 p.m.	**Dinner.** Plan for a big one as you will be amazed how hungry everyone is after such a strenuous day!
7:00 p.m.	**Opening Up.** Call everyone together and play an opening up exercise called Triad Booklets (page 71). Think through the best way to divide up the groups to facilitate your goals for the retreat. It is extremely beneficial to place a leader in each group to help set the tone and to help guide the discussion.
8:00 p.m.	**Debriefing.** Discuss the day's activities: 1. What gave you a real sense of accomplishment today? 2. What principles about life did you learn while rock climbing? 3. How does that apply to your relationship with God? 4. How does that apply to life back home? 5. How does what we did today relate to these verses: Psalm 121; Proverbs 3:5-6; Isaiah 26:3.
8:45 p.m.	**Discussion.** Talk about tomorrow's activities. Announce what time breakfast is and what everyone should wear for rafting.
9:00 p.m.	**Snack.** Build a campfire and have some Smores (a piece of chocolate and a roasted marshmallow between two graham crackers). Then do some singing.
10:00 p.m.	**Bedtime.** The youth should be tired out from the day's activities.

Day Three

7:30 a.m.	**Staff Meeting.** Discuss how your leaders feel the activities are going. Discuss any participants that have needs for some additional attention. Be sure the raft guides are there to discuss the day's schedule. Close with a prayer for the day's activities.
8:00 a.m.	**Rise and Shine.**
8:30 a.m.	**Breakfast.** Make sure to eat a hot breakfast as the river will be a bit cold and the youth will be able to use the additional warmth.
9:00 a.m.	**Devotions.**

9:30 a.m.	**Departure.** Meet the raft guides. See Whitewater Rafting (page 120).
Noon	**Lunch.** If possible, have the raft guides stop half-way down the river for lunch.
3:00 p.m.	**Arrival.** Arrive at the take-out spot. The group members will be very eager to change their clothes. Arrange beforehand to have the spare clothes in the vehicle that is at the take-out spot. At this point, the youth will probably be very tired. They also will be sunburned or cold (depending on the season you have this retreat). Have beverages available. Allow some free time to K.B.M.O. (kick back, mellow out). Play a game of Frisbee Football.
4:00 p.m.	**Debriefing.** Use the following questions to debrief the experience:

    1. Imagine that your life is a river flowing toward God. As you travel along the river in your raft, what is the big rock on which you keep getting hung up?

    2. What is your natural tendency when you get hung up on this "rock"? Why?

    3. What do you think God wants you to do when you hit the rock?

    4. What are three things you can do this week to make your trip down the river of life more successful? How can the group help you do these three things?

    As a final debriefing discuss "Where do we go from here?" Life is built on commitment to Christ, not just emotions. This retreat has been fun, but life isn't always. Discuss the parable of the house built on the rock, Matthew 7:24-27. The rock represents the Word of God, the sand represents emotions and untruths. Ask the participants for their insights to this passage.

5:00 p.m.	**Affirming.** Close the outing by doing Warm Fuzzies (page 90). Pack up all of your gear in the vehicles. Stop at a fast-food outlet for dinner on the way home.

The Week-Long Residence Camp, Snow Retreat, Urban Retreat, and Rock Climbing and Rafting Retreat are examples of retreats or camps that utilize the five-step process of building community. They are ready-made and easy-to-use ideas. Feel free to use or adapt them. Definitely use them as guidelines when you prepare your own retreat to build community in your youth group.

EPILOGUE

You have now worked through all five steps in the community building process: bond building, opening up, affirming, stretching, and deeper sharing and goal setting. Not only is your collection of individuals a *group* they are also a *force*. Their lives are in the process of change and they've become change agents in the lives of others as they share their love and faith.

That's the real purpose of this book: changed lives, action, difference in lifestyle. We, as authors, have tried to help you build a cohesive group. We've shared with you the five steps we've found helpful in building community and we have selected and developed exercises that create the climate for changed groups and changed lives.

There's an interesting factor that occurs in the universe: entropy. Webster defines it as "the degradation of the matter and energy in the universe to an ultimate state of inert uniformity." Sounds exciting, doesn't it! That means if we leave things as they are, they'll naturally degenerate. There's a pull toward mediocrity.

What does that mean for us? It means that we *always* will have to work at building community in our groups. Over a period of time, if left alone, group members will become less vulnerable with each other; less growth will result. We will need to keep working on the steps. Bond building exercises will be needed every so often. If the group stops sharing or a crisis of confidence develops, opening up exercises will be needed. We'll continually and consistently need to help group members in affirming. And we'll always need to keep working on stretching, and deeper sharing and goal setting, because those are areas most of us try to avoid.

In short, group building is never over. We're always in process. We can't move through the five steps once and say "Well, we've done that" and check it off our "ultimate" checklist.

Remember the words of Paul, "Therefore encourage one another and build one another up, just as you are doing" (1 Thessalonians 5:11). Encouraging one another and building one another up is a constant part of God's call to us in youth ministry.

Accept that call.

Make a commitment to be group builders forever!

Denny Rydberg
Ken Beebe
Robin Dursch

ABOUT THE AUTHORS

Denny Rydberg is the director of university ministries at University Presbyterian Church, Seattle. He is a widely respected youth ministry professional. For several years, he was vice president of Youth Specialties and editor of the Wittenburg Door. He's the author of several youth ministry resources including the **Serendipity Youth Bible Study Series**. He has a B.A. from Seattle Pacific University and has taken graduate-level courses from Western Washington University.

Ken Beebe is the director of marketing for Reachout Expeditions which utilizes wilderness camping to provide personal growth through group building. Ken develops promotional materials for Reachout Expeditions and is a mountaineering guide and youth counselor. He has a B.A. in sociology from George Fox College.

Robin Dursch is the program director for Reachout Expeditions. She programs all trips and supervises and trains the summer staff. Robin has helped with research and writing for the **Serendipity Youth Bible Study Series**. She has a B.S. in Christian education from Biola University.

Improve your youth ministry with . . .

Determining Needs in Your Youth Ministry

by Dr. Peter L. Benson and Dorothy L. Williams
Foreword by George Gallup, Jr.

Identify and respond to the specific needs and concerns of your young people. **Determining Needs in Your Youth Ministry** helps you zero in on the needs of any group of young people. Youth groups. Sunday school classes. Youth choir and more. Your complete survey kit includes . . .

- *20 surveys and answer sheets*
  (Each survey can be photocopied. You can offer this survey to any size youth group for years to come.)
- *Survey administration and scoring guide*
  (You'll get survey results fast. You'll administer the survey, score it and quickly determine the needs of your group.)
- *Interpretation guide*
  (You'll get keys for better understanding teenagers, your group and the results of the survey.)
- *Programming suggestions*
  (Then, you'll get step-by-step programs helping you meet the newly discovered needs in your group.)

Open new, positive lines of communication with your kids. And plan programming to better meet their needs with this professional ministry tool.

ISBN 0931529-56-5, $15.95

Youth Ministry Care Cards

Here's a quick, colorful and low-cost way to build attendance and give affirmation. **Youth Ministry Care Cards** are inspiring post cards your kids will love to get. Each card includes a meaningful Bible verse and zany cartoon.

Affirmations—positive, encouraging messages to let your kids know you're thinking about them.

Attendance Builders—unforgettable reminders to attract more kids to your meetings, retreats and special events.

Each 30-card pack contains 6 different messages.

Affirmations ISBN 0931529-28-X $3.95/pack
Attendance Builders ISBN 0931529-36-0 $3.95/pack

More . . . Group Retreats

Edited by Cindy S. Hansen

Bring your group closer together with proven retreats that focus on teenage issues. Choose from **30** carefully designed, ready-to-use retreats covering . . .

- Faith and commitment
- Stages of life
- Self-image
- School—plus 25 other important topics

Each retreat includes step-by-step instructions from start to finish. You'll get detailed time schedules, faith-building activities, inspiring devotional ideas and more. Discover new opportunities for spiritual growth with **More . . . Group Retreats**.

ISBN 093152912-3, $14.95

These and other Group products are available at your local Christian bookstore. Or order direct from the pubisher. Write Group, Box 481, Loveland, CO 80539. Please add $3 for postage/handling per order. Colorado residents add 3% sales tax.